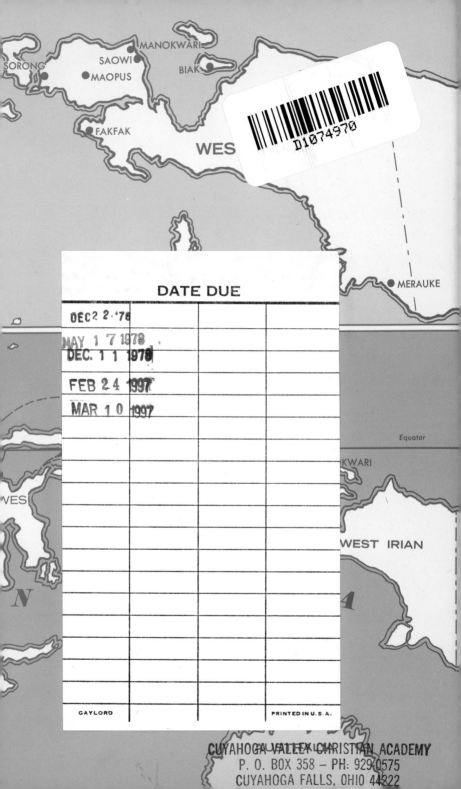

HOSTAGE
IN
DJAKARTA

HOSTAGE
IN
DJAKARTA

Harold Lovestrand

MOODY PRESS • CHICAGO

Dedicated
to
Those Intercessors Who Know and Value
the Power of Prayer,
Especially My Wife,
Muriel

Foreword

*Daily activity of thousands of missionaries quietly bear-*ing witness for Christ attracts little attention and is often taken for granted. But occasionally the Lord allows a missionary or a national believer to become the focal point of an intense spiritual battle where His own glory seems to be at stake. At times Satan apparently senses the possibility of easy victory. Then the lives of certain individuals become a spiritual battleground, as in the case of Job or Queen Esther.

During 1965 in Indonesia, Satan seemed to be planning a master stroke. It was evident that Communist Party leaders had plans to wipe out the leadership of the Christian churches there, including, if necessary, the slaughter of all who opposed them. The coup of October 1 came very close to victory, but the tide was turned and the Communist cause in Indonesia received a nearly fatal blow.

While these events were transpiring, God allowed His servant, Harold Lovestrand, to become not only a focal point of attack but also a focus for prevailing prayer. It may well be that an increased prayer burden for Lovestrand, languishing in solitary confinement in Djakarta, had a determinative effect on turning that tide.

To be caught up in history in the making is awesome and yet exciting. From the first news report which gave an inkling of trouble for an American missionary in Manokwari, West Irian, to the final act seven months later, Dr. Delbert Kuehl, TEAM's Executive Assistant Director, and I were deeply involved in contacts with the State Department, the families of the Lovestrands, supporting churches, interested friends and the news media. At the request of the State Department very little information reached the press lest the delicate negotiations be disturbed. I went to Djakarta during Harold's imprisonment. Though not able to see him, my interviews with American authorities were at least helpful in demonstrating our deep concern and also our confidence that God would answer prayer.

May Harold Lovestrand's story of political and spiritual conflict, of physical difficulty and personal testing while in a Djakarta prison, result in rich dividends for the work of God in Indonesia, particularly in West Irian where hundreds of tribes have yet to hear the gospel for the first time.

VERNON MORTENSON
General Director
The Evangelical Alliance Mission

Author's Acknowledgment

Grateful appreciation is expressed to David Woodward, TEAM missionary in Taipei, who gave professional assistance in preparing the manuscript for publication; to my beloved wife, Muriel, for her patient help in gathering much of the factual data; and to my uncle, Stanley Eriksen, who offered my family the use of his summer cottage at Mariaville, New York, where most of the manuscript was written. Thanks is also expressed to the various members of The Evangelical Alliance Mission staff for their advice and assistance, and to my numerous prayer partners, without whose prayers this book would not have been written.

HAROLD LOVESTRAND

CONTENTS

1

Don't Get Involved!

It was hot and sultry like most days on the New Guinea coast. The dull rumble of waves rolling on the seashore mingled with the call of wild birds. A few mountain people shuffled by on the coral road leading around the bay to Manokwari. There was nothing to mark the day as being unusual, yet I was on the threshold of a strange and torturous adventure.

A soft rap sounded at the front door, almost tentative in its gentleness. When I stepped to the door, I found four Papuan men standing outside. I recognized one, but the others were strangers.

Oh, I thought, *they've come to ask for gasoline like those who came last week. The stocks are all sold out in town, so they've come to the mission...*

Inviting them to enter the living room, I ushered them to rattan chairs. Then I waited for them to disclose the purpose of their visit. They looked at one another, as if deciding who should be the spokesman. A tall, thin man drew himself up and announced, "We have come to you to make a request."

Anticipating what he would say, I answered, "I'm sorry, but we have no gasoline to sell. I know that we have sold some once or twice in the past, but we have only enough for our own use now."

"No, no *Tuan*, ("sir")," he replied, "we are not interested in gasoline. You know how things are around here now. The people are dissatisfied. Many of them are out of work. You can't buy anything in the stores anymore. You can't even buy the necessities for living."

He stopped and looked at me to see how I was taking what he said. I just sat there without comment.

"You know how we Papuans have been treated since our country became part of Indonesia," he continued. "Things are different from when the Dutch were here. The people are not happy."

He paused. His three companions were watching me intently. "No," he said, "we don't want to buy gasoline, but we hear that you have a connection with the outside—ah—and—"

Light suddenly began to dawn. Now I understood what might lie behind their visit. I had a radio transceiver with which I kept in touch with many other stations in West Irian, the western half of the island of New Guinea. It was licensed and in routine use in this area. Were these men asking me to send a message somewhere for them?

"Wait a minute," I hastily interrupted. "If this request has any political connection, please don't make it. Don't say another word. We missionaries are not here to meddle in politics. We are here to preach about Jesus Christ to all men, and in this school of which I am an instructor we train others to preach the gospel. If we mixed in politics, it would mean the end of our work here; and we want to stay as long as possible."

"Well, *Tuan*, it is political," he admitted reluctantly.

"Then please don't bother to make your request," I said. "I don't want to have anything to do with politics, and I doubt if you should either. Let me try to explain why I say this."

I opened my Bible to the thirteenth chapter of Romans and read, "Let every soul be subject unto the higher powers. For there is no power but of God: the powers that be are ordained of God. Whosoever therefore resisteth the power, resisteth the ordinance of God" (Rom. 13:1-2).

My audience of four looked puzzled, so I enlarged on the verses, "We Christians cannot disobey God's Word, and it tells us to be obedient to our governors. Wouldn't it be better for you, too, if you would trust God about the present situation? I am sorry for you and your problems, but you should ask God to work them out. His way is always better than our own."

I prayed with the men; then they excused themselves and left. I watched for a moment as they walked off the campus. The Erikson-Tritt Bible School, which was named for the two martyred pioneer missionaries of The Evangelical Alliance Mission, was in the district of Saowi, thirteen kilometers from Manokwari. A party of Indonesian officials would soon be driving along that road to the airstrip near Saowi.

"It's time that I changed and got ready to go out to the airport, Honey!" I said to my wife. "Mr. Legowo is flying back to Djakarta this afternoon."

"Do you have to go? You're so busy," Muriel replied. "After all, you were at that meeting last night and saw him there."

"Yes, and I thought he sounded quite interested in having more schools develop here. I think the friendly thing for me to do is to see him off."

As I went to change my clothes I was thinking of Mr.

Legowo's speech the night before. His slow, emphatic Indonesian was somewhat didactic. Point by point he described how the government intended to transform West Irian into a progressive part of the republic. No longer would it be a backward colonial possession.

Mr. Legowo, who was second in command of the West Irian Affairs Office, had said, "The West Irians are now Indonesian citizens, and we will see to it that they are educated just as well as those in our public school system elsewhere. We have a responsibility to bring West Irian into the modern world."

He had been speaking to a gathering of school administrators and teachers. Missionaries conducting grammar schools and other educational work had been invited, and we had realized that this was a command performance. In his speech he referred to us, saying, "We need the help of the religious foreign missions in educating the people of this island. We urge you to continue your schools and to establish more of them, in cooperation, of course, with our educational authorities."

Knowing how the heavy hand of Communist indoctrination was being felt in all parts of Indonesia, we had some reservations about cooperation. It was one thing to comply with government standards and regulations; it would be something else again if radical socialism had to be taught in our schools. While a Bible school might not be quickly affected, we had an elementary school right on our campus.

While dressing I reflected on Mr. Legowo's words and actions. Wearing a lightweight suit to the airport would honor him but would not be too comfortable on a hot December afternoon in 1964. The airport from which he was leaving was not far away. It would only take me five minutes to get there in the Volkswagon Kombi.

Driving to the airfield, I was still thinking about the turmoil stirring this obscure corner of the world out of the lethargy of ages. Twenty years ago this area had been the center of bitter fighting in World War II. The jungle had not enveloped the camps and airstrips and the harbor wrecks had not rusted out of sight when the Dutch and Indonesians began to exchange acrimonious words about this piece of real estate which for centuries had remained wild and unwanted while other prizes were sought and claimed.

New Guinea had long been left to its stone age savages, colonial administrators, petty traders and a few missionaries. A revolutionary new nation changed all that. Indonesia would not be denied this part of the former Netherlands East Indies, and it had taken over West New Guinea and renamed it Irian Barat.

Near the airport entrance I passed the four men who had just visited me as they walked single file along the side of the road.

Strange, I mused, *that these four should come to see me the same day Legowo is leaving. Could there be any connection?*

My mind raced ahead: *Could he have sent them to me to feel out my opinions?* I dismissed the thought. This was the trouble about living in an environment subject to Communist influence. It created a police-state atmosphere, and it was difficult to take anyone at face value. *I'd better watch out,* I thought, *or I'll find myself looking under beds and jumping at shadows.*

At the airport the crowd of onlookers stood at a distance from the dignitaries. To my surprise Legowo and several of his companions were in uniform. Since police officials dressed almost exactly like army officers, this meant that Mr. Legowo could be related to security.

When I had an opportunity I spoke to Legowo, but he gave me a cool reception. When Komisaris Hardjanto, head of security for West Irian, acted the same way, I began to wonder. Then Franz Kaisepo, governor of West Irian and an old acquaintance of mine from days spent at Kokonao on the south coast, barely deigned to recognize me.

Something's up, I thought. *I wonder what the trouble is.*

I soon knew what part of the trouble was. That week the local Papuan police in Manokwari had mutinied. Their wages had been behind, and then they learned that they would not be granted the Christmas bonus which had been customary under the former Dutch government. First dissatisfied, then disgruntled, and finally feeling abused and tricked, some of them beat up the police chief and raided the police armory of its weapons.

The Indonesian armed forces quickly arrived on the scene from their camp on the edge of town, and a frigate of the Indonesian navy began shooting at them. Mortar fire added to the show of strength, and soon the rebels were ready to negotiate.

"We want our back pay," they insisted. When this was promised, they surrendered, realizing that continued resistance was useless in the face of such odds.

The military arrested the rebellion leaders, and outward peace was restored. From then on, however, the local police were only allowed to carry nightsticks as weapons. Driving past the military camp one day, I saw four prisoners out sunning themselves. I knew them for I had been in and around Manokwari for years. They waved to me like. old friends while their guards looked on.

During this time I visited the city mayor in order to arrange the transfer of some property. The mayor was a Papuan, and in the course of our conversation I reported how the four men had come to me and evidently had wanted to request something regarding our "outside connections" as missionaries.

"Perhaps they wanted you to send a letter outside the country for them, Mr. Lovestrand," he suggested. Then he suavely added, "It would be best for you if you do not get involved in any political affairs."

"You may be sure that I have no intention of doing so," was my reply. Somewhat startled by the very suggestion, I left his office in a thoughtful mood.

2

Turbulence Ahead?

*Between 1950 and 1952 Muriel and I had begun to dis-*cover for the first time some of the complications that political undercurrents make for ordinary people. We waited two years, first for Indonesian visas which never came and then for visas into Dutch New Guinea.

"I never had any idea what was going on out there in the Far East at the end of the war," I told my wife. "We fellows who were still serving in the military in the European theater were just thinking about coming home."

Neither of us had realized the intensity of the struggle then going on between the Dutch and Indonesians. By 1949 when my wife and I were in the final steps of training for the mission field, Dutch rule had ended in all but the territory of western New Guinea, and the red and white bars of the Republic of Indonesia waved over the other islands. The emergence of this great new nation captured the imagination of many young missionary candidates, but it proved extremely difficult to get there. Walter Erikson, the first TEAM missionary to go to Indonesia, found that it was also hard to stay. Since he was of Scandanavian origin and blond, he was frequently mistaken for a Dutchman. The resultant hostility was so serious that it became a question whether he could continue work. It was his decision to leave Indonesia and move eastward to New Guinea which led to the establishment of our mission's work there.

Ed Tritt followed him to the field after an exasperating wait in Singapore while the Dutch authorities made up their minds whether to grant him permission to enter this remnant of their former colonial empire. I myself had learned a lot during twelve years of missionary experience, at first under the Dutch administration and more recently with the Indonesian government. Indonesia had finally succeeded in its avowed aim of incorporating west New Guinea within its national boundaries. Years before we had tried repeatedly to enter the country but to no avail. Apparently if we could not go to Indonesia, Indonesia had come to us!

Once when the New Guinea question had been in the news and relations between Indonesia and the Netherlands were very ugly, war seemed imminent. Another missionary, who did not discount the danger, nevertheless advised us thus, "If you keep your eyes on the war clouds, you will never get any work done for the Lord."

Through trial and testing we had learned this truth. We did all that we could to meet the requirements of successive governments, making applications, filling out forms, abiding by regulations, securing licenses, paying duty, and conducting ourselves well as guests in another country. At the same time we did our best to ignore each subtle bid for us to enter into the clamor and criticism of the revolution going on around us.

Much as we sought to keep out of politics, the Indonesian government was determined to sound us out and discover how pliable we would be. The stronger

Communist influence grew the more it sought to control every aspect of the nation's life and even the strangers within its gates.

The West Irian Affairs Office surprised us by organizing a conference in Java to which it invited ninety-one missionaries and ten national church leaders, representing a cross section of Protestant and Catholic work. We would travel at government expense and be entertained in a resort hotel not far from the summer palace of President Sukarno at Bogor. This government-sponsored trip was scheduled for June, 1965.

The Evangelical Alliance Mission sent six missionaries and two national workers to these meetings. We Americans suspected that it would be a week of indoctrination, and we were not too wrong.

General Sutjipto, Komisaris Legowo, and their associates in Sekkib (the "West Irian Affairs Office") welcomed us warmly to Djakarta. We delegates were loaded on buses and given a motorcycle escort out of the city. Our hotel was bedecked with banners in our honor. It was a very auspicious beginning. Were we thirsty? Here were cold drinks. Did we need a little spending money for trinkets? This, too, could be supplied.

Of course, there was the business of the conference. We listened to interminable sessions in which we were briefed on the history of the revolution, the five points of the *Pantja Sila* (Indonesia's constitution), and suggestions on how we could cooperate with the programs of the government.

Mr. Sutjipto and Mr. Legowo seemed honestly interested in the progress of West Irian. It was with speakers like Mr. Subandrio and Mr. Njoto that we began to squirm. Mr. Subandrio as Minister of Foreign Affairs was known to promote close relations with Red China. Mr. Njoto was second highest in the Communist Party.

After Mr. Njoto had finished his speech a missionary rose and asked if he would answer a question. Mr. Njoto nodded his assent, and the missionary said, "One of the main points in the *Pantja Sila* on which this country is founded is belief in God. What is the Communist Party doing to foster belief in God?"

Mr. Njoto sputtered and turned the question to one side, but another missionary brought him back to the point, "Mr. Njoto, we still want to know your answer to the question. The *Pantja Sila* is regarded as the basis for all true patriotism in Indonesia. Belief in God is one of the five points. What is the Communist Party doing to foster belief in God?"

Mr. Njoto attempted to get off the subject, and then an aide whispered to him. He hurriedly picked up his papers and walked out, while the chairman of the meeting announced that Mr. Njoto had had to leave because of an appointment elsewhere.

During the "missionary conference" I wrote a spoofing letter to my parents to try and give them some idea of the fantastic propaganda I was hearing:

DEAR MOM AND POP,

I'm still in Java being indoctrinated to understand the socialism and revolution in Indonesia. Today we are hearing a member of the Communist party tell how Communism is the "feeling" of the Indonesian people!

We are also hearing about *Nasakom. Nas* stands for nationalism; *a* stands for *agama* or religion; *kom* stands for Communism. The present program of the country is to combine all three together to work for the revolution.

We have been hearing about all the imperialism of USA and the virtues of China and the other Communist nations. You see, it is not the people who are hated, but the capitalistic and imperialistic system.

It is such a shame that both of you have to sell your strength to the capitalists in order not to starve. It is no wonder you are not rich, for the capitalists have taken away from you what is really rightfully yours. I hope that there is some work for you to do, or I'm afraid you might starve before our next furlough. Now with Edna not working, Dave and she will have to struggle to keep from dying. Well, some day perhaps the socialistic world will be able to free all Americans from these evils.

We feel the need for much prayer these days . . . We see the need of turning over the work as quickly as possible to the national church . . .

During the conference Komisaris Hardjanto had been most helpful in securing entrance visas for my two oldest children, Tim and Andrea. They had been waiting in Manila for weeks to come back and spend the school vacation at home.

Just before they arrived in Djakarta, we delegates were received by President Sukarno himself at the summer palace. He described the aims and program of the Indonesian Revolution in phrases which were already familiar to us and then went on to urge us missionaries to have an active part in the revolution!

On my return to Saowi with Tim and Andrea, the other four children gave us a tumultuous welcome. I dropped my bags and stretched out my long frame on the settee. Muriel brought me some lemonade, and I thought I would relax. I was back in familiar surroundings, but could anything be the same again?

We kept up the small talk in front of the children, but when we were alone Muriel asked me, "How did it go, and what was it all about?"

"We were treated like VIPs," I replied. "Police escort, flags, colored lights, banners, and all that. But afterward there were the speeches and the literature. It is all tainted with Marxism. I'm really disturbed about it. I hadn't realized how Communism is growing and permeating every facet of Indonesian government. It is spreading into every walk of life. You know, Honey, it leaves me feeling that we don't have much time left to work here. I believe that the pro-Communists only intend to use missionaries as long as we are useful to them. After that they will get rid of us."

Muriel pushed back a stray lock of brown hair and sighed. "Do you really think it will be that bad?" she said. "Remember how worried we were when the Indonesian paratroopers were landing down the coast, and we thought they would fight the Dutch. There was the evacuation, and then everything settled down again. We came back, and things went on as usual."

I could remember well enough. Indonesia had been making an all-out attempt to force the Dutch to give up the island in 1962. We picked up news reports by transistor radio about paratroop landings. Then the Dutch evacuated their women and children and advised us to do the same. We finally decided to move women and children to our remote station up at the Anggi Lakes and await developments.

The morning they left was a memorable one. The word to evacuate came over our mission radio system only two hours before the plane was due. Muriel and the children rushed about, filling suitcases and getting things ready while the two single ladies, Marjorie Smith and Marilyn Traynor, helped pack the necessary food and household items. By noon their party had landed safely at the Anggi Lakes and that afternoon hiked the two-hour trail to our station at Trigdada.

For the next month the "fugitives," as they laughingly called themselves, kept house together. The crisp mountain air afforded them a much needed change from the humid heat down at Manokwari. Every morning found Muriel teaching our three oldest children, Tim, Andrea, and Joan, while the new missionaries, Marge and Marilyn, wrapped themselves in blankets to keep warm as they studied Indonesian. After the children were in bed in the evenings Muriel gave Indonesian classes to the other two. The three missionaries gathered around the wood stove while Muriel drilled the single ladies on Indonesian phrases.

Back in Manokwari I listened eagerly to the radio for news reports, hoping for some word concerning the outcome of the dispute. To maintain peace of mind I had to come back again and again to the Scripture which the Lord had impressed on our minds one day in our devotions before we had parted. It was a good cure for all uneasiness, for He had spoken to us through these words from I Peter 3:13-15, "And who is he that will harm you, if ye be followers of that which is good? But, and if ye suffer for righteousness' sake, happy are ye: and be not afraid of their terror, neither be troubled, but sanctify the Lord God in your hearts, and be ready always to give an answer to every man that asketh you a reason of the hope that is in you."

That was good medicine for this tense period. Although paratroopers continued to be dropped, there was no large-scale outbreak of fighting. Our area continued comparatively calm, and after a month in the lake region the women and children returned. As the emergency dissolved, other evacuees went back to their stations as well.

Missionary work had proceeded as usual, but in August, 1962, the Dutch announced that they would be leaving New Guinea and transferring the country to Indonesia. Almost immediately the Dutch population of Manokwari began to pack and leave for their homeland. From October to May of 1962 the country was under the administration of the United Nations Temporary Executive Authority. Then it became an integral part of Indonesia.

We left a month later for furlough in the United States, and it was not until our return that we got the full impact of the Communist influence which had extended into West Irian. Leaving our two oldest, Tim and Andrea, who had already started studying at Faith Academy in Manila, we winged our way down across the equator until we could see the steaming jungles and the blue mountain ranges of New Guinea again. New Guinea? No, we must learn to call it West Irian.

Manokwari seemed much the same outwardly, a scattering of tin roofs among the jungle green. The forest crowded right down to the sea where at low tide the salt flats lay exposed, smelling terribly. A small jetty—a freighter at anchor—the airstrip. We were home again, but what a difference we felt! No, the weather hadn't changed. It was the same as ever. Rather it was a psychological change which we sensed immediately. Our Papuan friends were more reserved. We saw uneasiness

written in their faces as well as caution on their
tongues.

Then we noticed a difference in the economy. The
bottom had virtually dropped out, and stores stood practically empty. The scarcity of jobs and even staple foods
had forced many to return to their villages in the interior
where they could at least cultivate gardens.

The other difference which affected us was the in-
crease in red tape. Within three days I had to fill out
registration forms with the Immigration Department, the
Public Prosecutor's Department, and the Intelligence Department of the police. From now on we would have to
carry police registration cards with us at all times. Moreover, if we wanted to go a distance of over fifty miles, we
would need a travel permit from the police. I learned that
it had become necessary to get permits and report on any
meetings other than the usual church services. The reports were supposed to summarize all subjects discussed
and decisions made.

After a year back in Indonesia I had adjusted to the
careful surveillance of our work. I knew from what some
of the officials told me that the Public Prosecutor's Department kept files on all of us foreigners. But when the main
government leadership in Djakarta tried to get us to support its socialist line, I was convinced that we were due for
further pressure.

I wasn't the only one of this opinion. In answer to
Muriel's question as to whether matters were in bad
shape, I replied, "Yes, worse than I had imagined. Mr.
Patterson from over on Biak has gone back from the
conference to pack up and leave. He and some others in
his mission say that they want to go while the going is
good."

3

The Law of the Jungle

---

*In the cool of the evening I reached over for my banjo-*ukulele and began to sing, first in English and then in Indonesian,

> What a Friend we have in Jesus,
> All our sins and griefs to bear;
> What a privilege to carry
> Everything to God in prayer.

Somehow that took the ache out of my heart. Poor Uncle Ariks! I had been thinking about him all day, ever since his tearful, red-eyed daughter had come to me with the news that the *Brimob* ("Mobile Police Brigade") had given him a severe beating.

Old Johan Ariks was a familiar sight in Manokwari as he slowly trudged the streets with his walking stick. As a retired schoolteacher, he was venerated by the people and some had been in his classes. He had even appeared before the queen in Holland, and now this man of honor had been humiliated!

It all started during the time I was attending the conference in Java. A group of Papuan leaders in Manokwari prepared a letter of protest and solicited signatures for it. This letter was addressed to the United Nations in New York, and it described their grievances in detail.

The bearer of the letter left for the other end of the island, planning to mail it from Australian territory. Word somehow reached the authorities about this, and he was arrested at Biak, only partway to his destination.

A wave of arrests followed, and after my return from Java I heard that Uncle Ariks was among those implicated. Terror swept through the town, and those who feared for their own safety fled to the jungle. Poor Uncle Ariks was at the mercy of the *Brimob*. They dared to beat a feeble old man, but they were wary of going into the jungle, which could be a place of death for them.

I knew something of the jungle and therefore had a respect for it and for its people. That was where some of these new officials and I differed. I was more at home in this land than they were, even though they called me a foreigner. Actually they were often confused by the Irianese and their ways. When they could not communicate with them or lacked the background to understand their thinking, they easily offended them. This led to suspicion. Suspicion led to fear, and fear to unwarranted brutality.

Not all of the officials were so unwise. There were men of education and gentility who deplored these excesses. It was not surprising that the new administrators would have misunderstandings with the local people. Even the old-time Dutch colonialists sometimes found them difficult to manage. That is why they were so slow about giving missionaries permission to open up new areas.

From the very beginning of our missionary career Muriel and I had been aware of the perils of the jungle. How could we forget the shock we received on our first trip out to New Guinea? Our ship sailed into the azure waters of Penang harbor in Malaya, and we looked forward to transshipping in Singapore for Djakarta. At breakfast we were handed a bundle of letters, and among them was a letter from TEAM headquarters. I tore open the envelope and drew out the contents—a glance and suddenly I felt weak and sick inside. Alarmed at my ashen features, Muriel asked me, "Harold, what's the matter?"

I couldn't reply. I couldn't say a word. In silence I handed her a news bulletin bearing the title, "These Gave Everything!" and the pictures of our good friends, Walter Erikson and Ed Tritt. Underneath was a copy of a cable received in Chicago from the S. S. "Hollandia":

> Deeply regret announced death by violence of missionaries Erikson and Tritt. Mutilated bodies found 17 October in river Ainim near village Maopas district Aifat subdivision Ajamaroe. Bodies interred on spot. Five native bearers suspected of murder arrested in meantime . . .
>
> GOVERNOR

What would their death mean to us? Would we be allowed by the Dutch to proceed to the field? Would we meet similar perils, and if so, how would we be able to overcome them in order to give the gospel message? All alone and without any advice from senior missionaries, how could we keep from making serious mistakes? These and other questions flooded our minds that sunny December morning in 1952.

Out on deck we continued to discuss the situation and committed it to the Lord. Immediately He answered with the assurance to our hearts that all would be well and that His grace was sufficient for our needs.

It was sobering for us as new missionaries to arrive in Manokwari and live in what had been Walter and Ed's home. We needed grace when we stepped inside the house in company with the Dutch district officer, F. R. J. Eibrink-Jansen. He had sealed it up, but it already was damp and musty. Cobwebs hung from the walls and ceilings. There were puddles of water on the floor and an accumulation of dust everywhere.

Friendly Mr. Eibrink-Jansen stroked his bald head for a moment and then said, "I have a solution for this mess. I'll send some prisoners up from the jail to help you clean house."

It was only later that we found that one member of the work crew had had a part in the murder of Walter and Ed!

We looked around our new home. It had been intended originally for a storehouse and consisted of a large room in the back, a smaller one in the front, and a bathroom. Along one side of the large room the men had stacked the prefabricated pieces of an aluminum house which they had planned to erect before our arrival on the field. It was the first and only time we ever lived with another whole house inside our house.

Our first days were filled with the details of making our home liveable, disposing of the personal effects of the two men, and getting used to life in this strange, new land. In front of our house lay a small, natural harbor, behind which rose the majestic Arfak Mountains, startlingly clear in the early morning and constantly changing hues during the course of a day.

Down the dusty road beside us trudged some of the

inhabitants of these very mountains, moving in single file—men clad only in loincloths, women wearing filthy sarongs, their matted hair braided and their faces carefully adorned with pig grease. Often they would stop and peer in our windows, intensely interested in our every activity.

At other times our visitors would be from the more civilized coastal tribes, clean and dressed, and with a good basic knowledge of the Indonesian language. Or sometimes we would welcome Eurasian people with a mixed background of Dutch and Indonesian, who preferred to be addressed in Dutch.

Tim, who was three years old at the time, heard us discussing which language to use with whom. "Mommy," he said. "I know—if they have shoes on, you say 'Good morning' in Dutch, but if they are barefoot, you use the local language."

Dutch was, of course, the official language in use when we arrived, and being able to speak it marked a person as educated. Our first close fellowship was with two groups of Eurasian Christians who met regularly for worship. Though the services were in Dutch and at first we could not understand a word, yet we felt our oneness in Christ. The bonds we had in common transcended the language barrier.

Many of our new-found friends had known the two martyred missionaries and had been blessed by their lives and ministry. Walter had often preached to one of these groups. Sundays always would find both young men walking to services two and a half miles away.

One day a man came up to me and said, "I knew Mr. Erikson when he was still living in a hotel in Hollandia. My friends and I called him 'the holy man.' When we had our wild parties, he would politely excuse himself. No matter how much noise we made at night he never complained. He often spent time alone in his room, reading and praying."

This had a profound effect on me. I longed to get out to the graves of these men and bring their bodies back to Manokwari for burial, believing that it would be an inspiration to missionaries yet to come.

When I confided in Mr. Eibrink-Jansen, he offered to go along with me; so we began to make plans. We looked into boat schedules as well as planes. We had lists of supplies and food to take. I arranged for an iron cross to be made, so I could plant it at the murder site.

Mr. Eibrink-Jansen accompanied me to Jefman Island and then to Sorong Doom, but then he found that he would have to return to Manokwari for unexpected business. A navy plane flew me alone up to the shallow Ajamaroe Lakes. A small raft scurried out to the waiting plane, and I disembarked. As we neared the small jetty I saw a Dutch couple waiting there. They were the Rev. Herbert Markus and his doctor wife, Dutch Reformed missionaries who extended to me the hospitality of their home. They insisted that the government *pesanggrahan* ("inn") was not up to the standard of the one at Sorong Doom, and I gladly went home with them.

That evening the district officer, Van der Veen, arrived unexpectedly with his young son. He had been out on a trek to the place where Erikson and Tritt were killed.

"My carriers have not arrived yet," he told us, "but they are bringing the hammocks, food, cameras, and other supplies of Erikson and Tritt. I even found Tritt's diary."

The news that we would have a day-by-day account of

their journey was exciting, and we hoped that it would give some additional clues as to what happened. The diary did confirm the facts which the Dutch authorities had collected. The two men had hired an armed guide and carriers to take them into the interior. It took the party three days of difficult climbing before they reached the Kebar, a grassy plain approximately 4,000 feet high. There they visited several villages, but when they wanted to go even farther the carriers became restive. They wanted to return home, and the guide, a man by the name of Jerimias Warijo, could not persuade them to stay. He hired some new carriers, and they continued their exploration. Sensing that Warijo might use his rifle to scare people in the villages they passed, the missionaries took it from him. He was deeply offended. Two days later as they bivouaced on the edge of the river Ainim, he struck back.

Walter and Ed had slung their hammocks close together, while the carriers made a rude shelter about fifty feet away. That evening they went to sleep while some of the carriers still chatted by the campfire. In the early hours of the morning Warijo crept up on the hammocks with one of the carriers, and with sharp machetes they savagely hacked away at the two missionaries.

The pastor surprised me by saying, "You will find Mr. Tritt's grave in the graveyard here. His body was thrown in the river, but the bones were recovered. The district officer brought them back after his first inspection trip to the scene of the crime. Would you like to see the grave?"

"Yes," I replied.

"Well, I'll send one of my houseboys with you to show you where it is," he said.

I followed the young Papuan and stood for a long time meditating at the spot he showed me. I prayed that I might live as these pioneers had lived and be as ready to die as they were.

The law of the jungle seems to be the survival of the fittest, but I didn't feel strong enough in myself to tackle its challenge. "The Lord is my Strength," I said to myself.

Back at the mission house I told the Markuses, "I'm going on in."

"I think that I'll go along, too," said the pastor.

"If you are going to go, I'm not going to stay here," his wife said. "I'm going along." And she did.

The Cross Marks the Spot

The porters hoisted their loads on their backs. One of them had the large iron cross on which the names of Walter Erikson and Ed Tritt were written under the heading, "Martyred for Christ."

We swung out along the trail, and I began my introduction to jungle life. Tramp, tramp, tramp for one day after another. The third day there was an all-day rain. I put on my pancho, but I soon discovered that it was useless. With it on I was so unbearably hot that perspiration soaked me through. With it off the steady rain kept me a sodden mess. The rain served to dampen the spirits of us all, and there was little talk as we slogged along. Gradually we spread out farther and farther from each other.

Toward the middle of the afternoon I was a little ahead of the rest of the party. At the end of a long climb, I sat down and pulled off a couple leeches. Suddenly I felt chilled, so I started walking again. Tired? Yes, I was tired, dead tired, but when I stopped walking I got cold. I lumbered slowly on my way, trying to move enough to keep warm but also slow enough so as not to get completely exhausted. Oh, how I longed for rest and warmth simultaneously!

Because of my dragging pace the others gradually
caught up with me, and it was a good thing, too. At this
point a huge tree blocked the trail, but there was a two-
foot-high tunnel through the underbrush where we could
squeeze by. Just after I crawled under the tree I felt a
searing pain in my left eye. I waited for Pastor Markus
and then begged him to look at my eye. He did, and
there he found my twenty first leech of the day. He took
two small twigs, and forming pincers, pulled the offending creature off my eyeball. Ten minutes later we reached
the shelter of a native house, and I gratefully slumped
down on the floor.

During the seventh day of our trek we reached the
village of Maopus, near the scene of the murders. Dr.
Markus stayed there to conduct a clinic while the pastor
and I pushed on. We followed the river Ainim up its
course, walking along its bank, hopping from stone to
stone, and sometimes wading in it.

At a sharp bend in the river we came up to a huge
rock, and one of the men pointed this out to us as the
place where Walter Erikson's body had been found by a
native woman. We climbed up the bank of the river at
this place, and there, thirty feet above the rushing water,
we found a grave covered with a thatched roof. This is
where the body of my fellow missionary lay.

"Let's go on to the campsite," I said to pastor Markus,
and we walked upstream another hour till we came to a
clearing. Our guide pointed out two trees which were
close together as the ones to which the heads of the
hammocks had been tied and from which they had been
stretched out in a V shape. I chose this spot to place the
iron cross, and we fastened the crossarms firmly to the
two tree trunks.

We had prayer beside the cross, and then I pulled out my camera to take some pictures. With this accomplished I turned to the pastor and said, "Let's return to the grave and exhume the body."

Up to this point I had been so busy that I concentrated on what I was doing, oblivious to how the porters felt. As we retraced our steps to the grave, they were very quiet and only talked in whispers.

"They are afraid of the spirits of the dead," the pastor told me.

It didn't sink in.

"Will you ask them to help me dig here?" I replied.

The men were reluctant to do so, but I insisted. In fact, I led the way. Digging down in the soft soil we soon came to a rude coffin of tree bark. I removed its cover. By this time the carriers were shuddering with fright and had drawn away from the grave.

Pastor Markus, who had been listening to what they were saying, came over to me. "You'd better stop," he said. "The men declare that they will not carry the remains out to the lake; they say that the spirits would be angry and would punish them."

Reluctantly I replaced the cover and began to shovel earth in over the coffin. I felt that I had failed in the main purpose of my trip.

The pastor saw my distress and tried to encourage me, "It would be better if you wait about two years until the flesh is gone and only the bones remain. By that time the natives' fear of the spirits will be much less, and you can make the transfer of the remains to Manokwari."

He was wise with years of experience, and I accepted his advice. It is best to learn from old hands, and later I made an eleven-day trek to this same spot. I secured the bones both here and at Ajamaroe and removed them to the coast. For the forty-five or so missionaries who have gone to TEAM's West Irian field the graves at Manokwari have been an inspiration, and I had the satisfaction of honoring the memory of my two friends.

On this first trip the pastor taught me much about the ways and thought patterns of the Papuans. I could see that he had the endurance, kindness and sense of humor needed to live with them.

One day when we were soaked with perspiration, he suggested that we bathe in a nearby small stream. A crowd of curious young boys followed us down to the water and stood around. I asked Markus if they were going to watch us.

"Oh, they're just curious," he replied. "I'll have them leave in a while."

When we had undressed, the sturdy Dutchman shouted at the boys, "Now that you see that we are white all over, you can go back to the village."

Obediently they turned and disappeared up the path.

Another day as the Markuses and I approached a group of huts we saw men and women arguing and gesticulating wildly. Some were running around shouting. The place was in an uproar. We pressed on to find out the difficulty. On one side we saw a gang of men standing around a stalwart young fellow whose back was to the wall. They were berating him while he stood calmly facing them, whittling a piece of wood with a razor-sharp knife.

On inquiry we learned that he had just married a second wife. His first wife naturally was intensely jealous, and in a fit of temper she had drunk poison to end her life. Now she was fearful, knowing that she would die. She ran around the village screaming while her relatives threatened the husband. He kept on carving away on his switch.

Dr. Markus began giving orders. "Bring that screaming woman here immediately. Mantri, get some soap. Bring warm water. Bring me some ashes."

In a few moments Dr. Markus had a potion ready and gave the young wife an emetic. Before long she lost the contents of her stomach and was out of danger. At that, the commotion subsided, but even later that night we heard the occasional outburst from the lips of some offended relative.

The young Papuans who had ambition to become more civilized were torn between the new and the old. Back in Manokwari where I started a Bible study class for young men, I came one night to the church to find a warm discussion in process. I inquired what it was all about, and a young fellow named Lambert told me his story.

"We are talking about some of our customs," he said. "This month when I received my pay, I went to the store and bought myself a nice pair of long pants. When I wore them home, my uncle was in the house. He said, 'Lambert, I like those pants. Give them to me.' So I had to give my new pants to my uncle."

"Why?" I asked.

"*Tuan*, it is this way. It is the custom of the tribe," he answered. "Whenever someone older and more respected asks another person for something, he must give it to him or else he will have to leave the village."

"What do the rest of you think about this custom?"

Lambert answered for them, "My friends here don't

think that the custom is right. Here I work all month to get that money, and when I buy the pants, my uncle gets them. He doesn't work. All he does is sit around the house. I work, and he gets the reward. This isn't right. It makes me feel like quitting work. This isn't justice. The man who works does not receive his reward. We think this custom is very damaging for us young men. How can we advance ourselves when all that we work for is taken away from us? What do you think about this custom, *Tuan?*"

"Well," I ventured, "it does sound unfair."

"It is unfair," he replied. "Do you know what I'm going to do? I'm going back to my uncle and demand that he give them back. I don't care if I am thrown out of the village. This custom ought to be stopped, and I'm going to fight against it. I'm going to go back and say, 'Uncle, I want those pants back. Your taking them is just like stealing. I demand my pants back.'"

At the next class meeting I asked Lambert, "Did you get your pants back?"

"No," he replied ruefully, "when I asked my uncle for the pants, he said, 'What a pity! Your grandfather saw me wearing those pants, and he asked me for them. Now he has them.'"

Lambert hadn't pursued his pants any further, but he did follow after the Lord Jesus Christ. Experiences like his added to my understanding and love for the Papuans. As more missionaries arrived and TEAM's work spread out to the Bird's Head region to the west, we came in contact with many different tribal types. Some of the tribes on the south coast were so fierce and cannibalistic that the government was most unwilling for missionaries to approach them.

The restrictions placed on us by the Dutch government were often for our own good. For instance, a new missionary couple would not receive their entrance visas unless we had built and prepared a house for them to live in. As we began to stake out new stations, government regulations required that we carry a radio transmitter with us on trek in order to keep in touch with our home base. Missionary Aviation Fellowship came to New Guinea to help the various missions with the problem of transportation. With air service available to the most remote points we began aerial surveys, counting villages or tree houses in order to determine population density. Then the choice of a station site would be determined by the availability of suitable space for an airstrip.

Jack Manly, Charles Preston and Forrest Thorsby engaged in some of this early exploration. After they discovered the Testega location, Forrest and Dorothy Thorsby traveled in to take up residence in the unfinished makeshift house prepared for them. At the end of ten days walking over treacherous mountain trails they arrived at the little shack which they improved with a tent and gunnysacks. Future missionaries had better quarters right from the beginning because MAF airdrops brought in building materials and supplies.

With more missionaries coming it became apparent that as a mission we needed a base of operations in the Manokwari area. We secured the Saowi property, and Chuck Preston and I began construction of the first buildings there. From early morning until midafternoon we led a group of laborers in clearing trees, making roads, hauling cement and sand, and after that we came home to Manokwari to clean up for our evening Bible classes.

Gradually Saowi developed into a major staging area where we had missionary residences and apartments as well as a warehouse to store mission and personal property.

When the Erikson-Tritt Bible Institute was opened, Saowi was the most suitable location for it. The campus was not isolated, for it had the airport on one side of it and an army post on the other.

Part of our schooling as missionaries was to learn to wait—waiting for mail, waiting for supplies, waiting for permissions, waiting for suitable weather while we longed to be on the move.

In the spring of 1955 Chuck Preston and I surveyed the south coast, particularly the two main centers of Kokonao and Agats. The first was the region of the Mimikas, a tribe of about 8,000 scattered along the rivers in thirty villages. Farther south lay the government post of Agats, serving the cannibal tribe of the Asmats. We were startled to find the men here completely naked except for bone ornaments stuck through their nostrils!

Chuck and Calvin Roesler built a home for their families at Ajam, twenty-five miles upstream from Agats. On the day that their wives left Manokwari to join them, the villagers of Ajam went on the warpath. They killed twenty-nine people and brought their bodies back for a cannibal feast. Chuck and Calvin watched out the windows of their partially completed house as the women of Ajam danced in celebration of the victory, waving the skulls of the victims. A few days later the missionary wives arrived on the scene, rejoicing that the authorities had not been able to cancel their coming because they were already on the way. The two couples did not need to be convinced that the Asmats needed to know Jesus Christ!

Kokonao became my parish for several years. All the houses there were built up on stilts because of tidal flooding during certain seasons. During the floods even wild creatures might seek refuge in the homes.

One night my daughter Joan woke us calling, "Daddy, Daddy! There's a pig in the house."

I took my flashlight and looked everywhere, but I found nothing. When I tried to settle Joan back down, she said, "I heard it. I know I did."

A little later she woke me a second time with her cry, "Daddy, come here! There's a pig in the house!"

My second search revealed nothing, but Joan would not be reassured. Finally I lay down beside her and told her to go to sleep. The next thing I knew she was poking me, and I heard a merry laugh. "Daddy," she said, "there is a pig, and it's right here in bed with me!"

I realized that I had been snoring, and the problem was solved.

5

Emergency Call

Midmorning chapel service at the Bible school was in progress in the dining hall. The students sat around tables with their Bibles and hymnbooks in front of them. I sat back and viewed the group with considerable satisfaction.

On our third term of service we had not been reassigned to Kokonao but had returned to Bible teaching at Saowi. These students came from eight different language groups, but we taught classes in Indonesian.

Two of my former students, Akwila and Martin, were now working side by side with me on the teaching staff. With their families they occupied what had been missionary residences, and our weekly teachers' prayer meeting was held in rotation in all our homes.

As the chapel period ended Bob Lenz and I noticed a curious thing.

The students, instead of getting ready for the next class, were gathered together with the national teachers. The whole group was talking loudly to one another. Finally one of the students detached himself and came over to me.

"*Tuan*," he addressed me earnestly, "tomorrow morning at four o'clock there is going to be a revolt. The men

who are hiding in the jungle are going to att
Indonesian forces."

Some other students came over. "Yes, *Tuan,* that's
what they are going to do," they chimed in. "They are
going to attack the army post in town and the camp out
here."

I shook my head in disbelief. "How could this happen?" I said. "What would they fight with? Bows and
arrows? Machetes? Knives? You know the Indonesian
army has modern weapons. The men in the jungle
wouldn't stand a chance."

"But they are going to fight. They've been preparing."

"I don't see how they could imagine winning," I
answered.

"But they are going to fight, and that means the
fighting will be right around here," they told me.

Mr. Lenz and I refused to take their talk seriously, but
we could see that they were frightened.

"We want to go to the jungle and hide," they told me.
"This is a very bad place to be because we are next to the
main road."

"Why don't you wait a while and see?" I suggested.

"No, then it will be too late for us to get away. We
need to go now. May we go and pack our things?"

From the confusion and concern among them I could
see that it was pointless to attempt further classes that
day. All this month of July, 1965, rumors had been
circulating that there would be a Papuan revolt against
the government. This had evidently worked up the student body to a fever pitch.

I made an on-the-spot decision, "If you are determined to leave, why don't you go to the school garden

and camp there? It's not far away, and if there is any shooting you will be out of range. If there is trouble, you can easily go deeper into the jungle."

This seemed to satisfy them, and I assumed that we could resume classes the next day.

Leaving chapel I headed across campus for home. Muriel looked up from her class with our children with surprise. "What brings you home so early?" she asked.

"The students are all stirred up by a rumor that a rebellion will break out at four o'clock tomorrow morning," I explained. "They are sure that the Bible school will be right in the middle of the shooting. Can you imagine that?"

"No, but do you think that there is any sort of preparation which we ought to make?"

"We're as safe here as anywhere," I replied. "And besides, I can't see how the Papuans could possibly tackle the army."

I informed Muriel of the permission I had granted the students to move to the garden patch fifteen minutes' walk away. By that evening all but three of the students had fled. The evening seemed quieter than usual with no life stirring on the campus. The shadows deepened, and the stars came out. We went to bed wondering, just wondering if anything would really happen.

I awoke to find my wife shaking me. "Harold, Harold, wake up," she said. "Someone is knocking at the door."

Sure enough I could hear knocking. I turned on my flashlight and looked at my watch. It was ten minutes to two. Who would be wanting us at that time of night?

I went to the door and found Akwila there.

"*Tuan*," he said breathlessly, "Amon is badly hurt. He is bleeding a lot."

"Where is he?" I asked.

"We took him over to Mrs. Lenz, and she is fixing a bandage."

"What happened to him?"

"The boys didn't stay at the garden. They went on into the jungle, and in the dark Amon slipped. He fell into a hole and ripped his cheek open on the coral rock."

I knew that jagged coral! The hills back of us had at one time been under the sea, and we often had picked up fossil seashells there.

Akwila continued his story, "The boys say this happened about ten o'clock. It has taken all this time to carry him back. Mrs. Lenz says that we should get him to the hospital quickly. Can you take him?"

"If he's badly hurt I don't think that he could ride on the back of the Vespa," I answered. "Maybe I could go to the airstrip and call for an ambulance from there. Let me get dressed, and I'll be right out."

Mrs. Lenz handled our school dispensary, and if she recommended the hospital it must be because Amon's injury was more serious than she could handle.

Soon I rejoined Akwila, asking him, "Do you want to go along?"

"Yes," he answered, and the two of us buzzed off down the road. Just before we reached the turn into the airport, we were stopped by a waving flashlight. A squad of armed Indonesian soldiers surrounded us.

"Where are you going, and what are you doing this time of night?" the squad leader demanded.

"I am on my way to the airport to use the telephone," I said. "One of the students at Saowi fell into a deep hole and has torn open his cheek. He needs to go to the hospital. I want to call for the ambulance!"

The leader lowered his rifle slightly. "All right, you may go to the telephone," he said. "You!" he added, motioning to Akwila, "Come with us!"

He took him away for questioning as I went to the phone. It was dead. I could get no connection. What should I do? Then I remembered that the airport manager had a switch in his home from which calls were handled after hours. He was a Christian from North Sulawesi, and I felt he would not mind being wakened in the middle of the night for such an emergency.

"The line is dead," I told the soldiers who were watching me. "I must go over to the manager's house."

They trailed me over to his place. There I knocked until he responded. Soon I was speaking to the night duty desk at the Manokwari Hospital, and the nurse there promised to send the ambulance at once.

"Thank you," I told the manager and then went outside to wait. The squad leader came along and went in the manager's house to call his headquarters.

In less than half an hour the ambulance reached the airport, and I put my hand on my scooter, expecting to lead the ambulance to the Lenz' home.

"No, you'll have to wait," the soldiers said. When I looked surprised, one of them explained, "Headquarters is sending a vehicle out to investigate, and you'll have to wait until it comes."

"Can't the ambulance go ahead of me?" I asked.

"No, it will have to wait here."

I passed another half hour under the stars, rather restive that there should be such a delay in getting help to Amon.

At last a Volkswagen Kombi arrived, filled with soldiers. One of them began to discuss the situation in low tones with the squad leader, and he came over to me. "All right," he said. "You can go with the ambulance to Saowi to get the injured man, and we'll watch your motor scooter."

Taken aback, I replied, "I prefer to go back to Saowi on my scooter and show the ambulance the way."

"No," he replied, "you can get your scooter when you come back."

I was uncertain whether to believe him or not. It sounded incredible that I couldn't drive off on my own machine.

"Look," I said, "you know that I'm a citizen of another country. If you want to get me for further questioning, you can always find me at Saowi. I want to get back to my wife and children."

This caused further consultation until he returned to me with a gesture of dismissal, "You may go on your scooter, but be sure you stay with the ambulance and the military car."

As I putted down the road in the headlight glare of my convoy, I wondered what had happened to Amon. Would it be too late to get him to the hospital? We found him weak but still alive and lifted him into the amublance. It roared off down the road, the Volkswagen Kombi in pursuit, and we missionaries were left alone.

When I crawled back into bed, it was about 3:30 A.M.

"They held Akwila at the airfield for questioning," I told Muriel. "Even after all that time of waiting, they weren't through with him. I wonder why those soldiers are acting so fussy."

6

In Confederate Territory

Just before dawn my wife and I awoke to the sound of shooting. I sat up in bed. "It's really happened!" I said. "The Papuans have rebelled."

"Where is it coming from?" Muriel asked.

I listened carefully, then said, "I think it's over in the direction of the army post. They've launched an attack on the camp."

The firing continued for about half an hour, and then it slackened. Muriel and I had our private devotions, dressed, and started the day like any other. The children had not heard the rifle fire and did not know that anything was amiss.

I went over to my transmitter at 7:45 A.M. for the regular radio schedule with the interior stations. When I got hold of Calvin Roesler, the field chairman, I told him, "I think we'd better cancel the field council meetings which are scheduled here in Manokwari."

"Why is that?" he asked with surprise in his voice.

"There is an altercation up here between the Confederates and the Yankees," I replied. "We appear to be in Confederate territory."

"OK," he answered and didn't probe further. "We'll have to get in touch with MAF and tell them that we won't be needing their plane."

I listened to the other TEAM traffic over the receiver and then turned off the radio.

Just as classes were due to begin Ron Hill drove up from Manokwari. "I'm sorry you've had to make the trip out, Ron," I told him. "We'll not have any school today. There are no students for you to teach."

I began to explain to him what had happened, but as Ron, Muriel, and I stood there at the front of my house, our dog Rover began to bark furiously at the rear. I hurried to the back door to see what the trouble was. The dog was keeping a big, strapping Papuan rebel at bay. The man was dressed in green fatigues and held a rifle fixed with a bayonet.

He stood by a tree, looking a little tense and perplexed. I called the dog off, and he turned toward the cacao grove next to my house and signaled. Three companions stepped out of cover, one of them armed with bow and arrows, another with a machete and the third with a lead pipe!

The big man in charge asked me, "Have you seen any of my companions?"

"No," I answered, shaking my head.

"I was wondering if any of them had passed this way," he said. "We are on our way to Manokwari, and somehow we have to stop traffic between the Arfai army post and the camp in town."

With that remark he led his band off into the jungle that bordered us so closely. For my part I rushed back to Ron and told him, "If you want to get back into town, you'd better go while you can. I just saw four rebels at the back, and they said they intend to block the road between here and Manokwari."

Ron made a quick exit and headed back for town. About an hour later Rover began barking fiercely again. This time when I went to the back door I saw a group of five rebels. I told Rover to be quiet, and a tall, lanky Papuan stepped up. He sported a pistol strapped to the side of his green fatigue uniform, the same type of weapon the military police usually wore.

"Have you seen any of my companions?" he inquired.

"Yes," I answered. "I saw four. One was a big, husky man. He said they were heading for Manokwari, and that they intended to block the road in between."

They filed off, the one with the pistol, two with bows and arrows, one with a machete, and another apparently unarmed but busy chewing on a piece of sugarcane! As I looked at them disappearing through the tall grass, I thought they presented a rather pathetic picture of homegrown patriots.

About eleven in the morning some local Saowi residents came by. Seeing Muriel, they called to her, "The bridge has been destroyed. We could walk across, but cars cannot pass."

This bridge was just three or four hundred yards down the road from the Bible school. At 2 P.M. we heard small arms gunfire in the direction of the bridge, and we wondered how the Lenz family were faring because they lived close to it. When things quieted down, I hopped on my scooter and went down to their house.

Bob looked a bit nervous. He had been able to see the skirmish as an army jeep approached from Manokwari and was ambushed by the rebels.

On my return across the campus I made the rounds of the school buildings and found that fifteen of the students had returned. While I was talking to them, a platoon of Indonesian soldiers crept up on us, looking for rebels. I shouted to them, "You don't have to be afraid of anything here at the school. There are no rebels here."

The lieutenant in charge came up to me. "Call your students together," he ordered. "I want to have a talk with them."

I called the boys, and they gathered together on the grass in back of the dining hall. The soldiers surrounded them, holding their rifles ready.

The lieutenant began: "Some irresponsible men made an attack on the army post this morning. Twenty-three men died in the fighting, some of our men, and some of the rebels."

He looked around at the group. "The bridge over the Saowi River was also damaged. I hope that none of you had anything to do with that."

"We didn't. We didn't," chorused the students.

"Well, good. I hope that you are responsible young men and will demonstrate that you are loyal Indonesians. If that bridge is damaged again, I'm going to hold you responsible. And if you hear anything, you report it immediately to the post commander, or you can report it to your teacher," and he pointed at me. "Your teacher can report it to the army commander at Arfai," he continued.

While he lectured, one student was careless enough to look over his shoulder. "Hey you, pay attention!" a soldier shouted, pointing his rifle at him.

The students cowered together and were obviously relieved when the lieutenant and his detachment moved on.

"Shall we go fishing this afternoon, *Tuan?*" they asked me, for they often went spearfishing for food.

"No, I think the less we move around the better," I told them. This 28th of July had had more than its share of excitement.

After a peaceful night the happenings of the previous day hardly seemed possible. At our regular radio schedule I was very cheerful with Cal Roesler. "Things seem to have calmed down," I reported. "Since we already have government clearance for the field council meetings and the flights are already on the MAF schedule, I think that we might as well go ahead with the meetings."

"OK," he said. "We'll move your way."

Little did I know that at that very moment the rebels were attacking a section of the town of Manokwari!

This was July 29, and it also saw renewed fighting near the campus. A racket started during siesta time, and I told our children to stay in bed. Lying down, they were protected by the walls of our cement block house, and the firing was so close that stray bullets might come our way. This time the exchange of lead lasted longer than it had the day before.

A while later a convoy of military trucks passed our house in slow procession. Soldiers were walking along in front, between the trucks, and at the end of the line. Others were riding. They all looked skittish and overwrought, glancing from side to side for snipers. It must have been with good reason, for some of the windshields in the vehicles were shattered.

Half an hour later I heard more shooting. I judged that it was near the airport. Soon afterward I happened to turn on some water, and the pressure was low.

"Muriel," I called, "we'll have to start collecting water

immediately. I think the rebels have cut the water supply."

I proceeded to fill an empty fifty-five-gallon drum, two wash tubs, and some pails, glad to have caught that much of a supply while the water was still running. It stopped eventually, but I discovered that I could siphon out all the water we needed from our lowest outside tap. During the next days this source never failed even though the army camp and airport were without water.

The third morning I heard the TEAM schedule at the regular hour. This was July 30, and I learned that the field council members from the south coast were already in the air and on their way.

I hopped on my scooter and started toward the airport. When I came to the bridge, I found that the Indonesian army had repaired it, replacing the planks which the rebels had ripped out.

By the time I arrived at the strip the MAF Cessna aircraft was already down on the ground and refueling. Dave Peel, the pilot, was tending to the plane, but Cal Roesler and Dr. Kenneth Dresser were eagerly waiting for me.

"Tell us what's been going on here," they demanded, and I proceeded to brief them on our local war.

7

Clean Sweep

"I wonder why Ron hasn't come out yet from Manok-wari," I said. "He should be here with the supplies and mail for the mountain stations."

I looked at the soldiers who had gathered around the MAF aircraft, curious to see what was going on.

Dave Peel walked over to the office to check out, and in a few minutes he came back, shaking his head. "The fellow in there won't give me permission to take off," he said. "He says that he doesn't have any authorizations for plane movements. I told him that if I didn't leave before ten o'clock I wouldn't be able to land on that one-way strip at Anggi."

I knew what he meant. By midday it could cloud up at some of the inland stations, and often the wind would reverse itself completely, making it impossible for a plane to land.

Going over to the telephone, I found it in use. An officer was trying to make the connection with his superiors in town, but the lines seemed to be fouled up. As I stood there, two Papuans came in from outside. They sat down heavily on a bench and wiped the perspiration from their foreheads.

"Whew!" one of them said.

"What have you been doing?" I asked.

"Digging a grave!" was the reply.

"A grave! For whom?"

"It is for the uncle of the Saowi chief. You must know him. He was deaf but a good worker. Yesterday when the army patrol came by from Arfai, he was out cutting grass in front of one of the houses here. He was frightened when he saw the soldiers coming, and he started for a house. They hollered for him to stop, but, of course, he couldn't hear a thing. He only got a few yards before he was cut down."

He stretched himself wearily, "As soon as the grave is deep enough and we get boards for a coffin from town, we will bury him."

"That must have been the burst of shots I heard yesterday afternoon," I exclaimed. "The convoy went by the school, and after a while I heard firing. I thought it came from near the airport!"

We lapsed into silence. After a delay of about half an hour I said to the soldier at the telephone, "Look, you're not getting through, but if the plane waits any longer the winds will be too strong in the interior for the pilot to land. Why don't you let him go, and he'll return in about an hour? Perhaps by that time you will have permission for him to leave for his home base in Nabire."

He looked doubtful, but I added another argument, "That's a doctor who is going in with him. He has a serious case at Anggi Lakes and needs to get there."

At that he consulted off to one side with another soldier and then granted permission for Dave to take off with Dr. Dresser. I hurried over to the plane to tell Dave. "Ron hasn't come yet with the rice and mail," I added.

"We'll have to forget it this time and take it in when

Dick Griffiths returns after your field council meetings," he said. "Come along, Doc. Let's get going!"

Cal and I watched the plane rev up and depart. When it was out of sight, I said to Cal, "It doesn't look like Ron is going to get here. I'll take you out to Saowi on the Vespa scooter."

An hour later I was back at the airport to greet the plane again. While waiting for it, I went over to the transmitter house to see if permission had come through for Dave to return to his home base at Nabire. Nothing had come, but when the plane arrived with the other field council members, we managed to get through to the chief of police in Manokwari. He took responsibility for letting the MAF plane leave.

Ron still had not come from town, and I began to ferry the men over to Saowi. It took several trips, and on one of them I noticed how the telephone lines were hanging close to the ground, temporarily connected after having been severed by the rebels.

The next day the visiting missionaries presented their travel documents to the police department. There the men were informed that they would have to move into Manokwari for the meetings.

"But we have permission to hold our meetings at Saowi," they objected.

"That was before; now you must come in to Manokwari," was the answer.

Where was Ronald Hill and what had happened to him? We found him at home and heard his story. The day before he had loaded up the Volkswagen Kombi with the air cargo, and he had started out with his son Mike to meet the plane. Driving through the town, he was stopped by a military guard who came over to inspect the car. When he saw the sacks of rice in the vehicle, he whipped out his pistol.

"You're taking food supplies to the rebels," he declared. "I'm taking you to headquarters."

He forced him to drive to the army camp in Manokwari and from there to police headquarters. He was barraged with questions while Mike waited patiently outside in the car.

During this period of interrogation Ron looked up and saw Akwila passing by with a guard. A little while later he saw the teacher returning. They made no attempt to communicate with one another, but their glance expressed mutual sympathy for each other. Akwila strode along relaxed and erect. Evidently he was holding up well.

"They made me sign a statement before they released me," Ron told us. "This will be some experience for Mike to tell about when he goes back to school in Formosa."

He went out to the campus in the afternoon and brought the men's suitcases back with him. Field council meetings commenced and ran through the first days of August. We were much in prayer for Akwila, for the students, and for ourselves. What should we do about the Bible school? Should we carry on? This seemed unlikely.

Two students returning from the school garden had been accosted by a patrol of soldiers. They had a wheelbarrow of cassava roots which they had just dug up. They were frisked for weapons, and their machetes were seized.

The path lay alongside the Saowi River, and the soldiers flung these knives into the water. "You fellows watch out," they threatened. "If anything more happens to the bridge down there, we'll sweep you clean with our machine guns."

Other soldiers passing through the campus echoed the same warning to the students, "If that bridge is destroyed, we'll come here and sweep you all clean!"

The students reported this to me, saying, "We want to leave; we want to go back to our homes."

We discussed in field council the possibility of moving the school to Menjamboo where there was enough housing for them. Another course of action would be to assign the students to various stations for a period of practical work. Someone mentioned that we ought to have police approval if we closed the school.

Shooting continued sporadically, and two Indonesian air force planes flew over the jungle, trying to spot and destroy the rebels. One of these was an old World War II Mitchell bomber.

Back at Saowi I found the students in a state of nerves. Was there anything I could do to calm them and save the school? Perhaps if I made an appeal to the commander at Arfai, he would consent to caution his men about scaring our students.

I drove over to the army post, and a guard halted me at the gate.

"I would like to speak with your major," I said. He checked on this for me, and a lieutenant came out to see what I wanted. I explained the frame of mind the boys at school were in and asked if a more peaceful relationship could be worked out between the soldiers and the students. The lieutenant told me to wait by the Volkswagon Kombi which I was driving, and then in half an hour he came back with the major.

"Get into line with our vehicles," the major ordered. "We are going in to Manokwari."

"It is late in the day, and I need to get home," I said.

"You come with us," he replied curtly.

We passed my house on the way in, and I leaned hard on the horn. My sons, Stevie and Dan, were in the yard and saw me go by. This was all I wanted. They knew I was going to town, and, of course, they would tell their mother.

What followed was unpleasant and tiring. I was interrogated all through the evening at the army camp in town, shifted around from one officer to another. This went on until three o'clock in the morning when the military escorted me over to the police compound. There I faced further questioning. At the end of another hour my police interrogator said, "You can go now, but we can't take you back to Saowi. It is too dangerous to travel that road at night. We'll take you to your mission home here in Manokwari."

Ron Hill was completely surprised when I woke him up from a sound sleep, but he helpfully put up an extra cot and strung a mosquito net for me. I lay down exhausted but too high strung for sleep. My head echoed and reechoed with words, words, words.

The men gathered around me in the morning, and I explained what I had been through. I tried to shrug it off, but my mind was settled on the school question. It would have to close.

The next days we were busy making arrangements for students to travel home. We were able to put a number on a passing ship, and this meant two trips in from the school with the Kombi packed with the boys. The second time I passed the airfield entrance I was stopped by suspicious guards. "What are all these men you are carrying?" they asked. They were not too satisfied with my answer.

I was glad when the field council adjourned. Returning to the deserted campus, I told Muriel, "Tomorrow I'll have to take my minutes of the meetings and file them with the police, and then I'll be able to stay here in Saowi. No more going back and forth to Manokwari. Every time I go the airport guards scowl at me."

"I'll be glad to have you back," she said. "It is just a bit too much for me."

I felt a rush of sympathy for her, knowing that she had been through a week of tension. One day an army patrol had come along and asked her if there were any paths from the campus leading into the jungle.

She had said, "Yes."

They had asked, "Where?"

Not thinking, she called to Danny and said, "You show them the path over there," not realizing that they would take him with them into the jungle. When they all disappeared, she called after them frantically. All she could think was, *What if they come across some rebels with Danny leading the way?*

The patrol did not advance very far into the jungle, and before long they reappeared with Danny. Maybe they had their own qualms about meeting the rebels, but Muriel felt that she had had just about enough of both soldiers and rebels.

She broke a long pause, saying, "I know something that you don't, and I don't think that I ought to tell you."

I gaped at her. "Not tell me?" I said. "Why is that?"

"I think it's better that you don't know," she said cryptically.

I understood. The less I knew the easier it would be with police questioning.

8

Saowi Over and Out

The military had been coming and going all during this period of the rebellion. Sometimes they set up their machine guns in front of our house. This was entertaining for the children, but it was nerve-racking for Muriel and the other missionaries. Doris Taylor, a new arrival from the States, was living in a house with walls of only hardboard, and she usually slept in our house in order to be safe in case of shooting.

What Muriel told me much later was that one day when she had been giving Doris a language class, a knock sounded at the back door. Muriel went back and found a mountain chief whom she recognized. He looked around to be sure that no one was watching. Then he reached into his pocket and pulled out a folded piece of paper. He handed this to her.

"Here's a letter from the jungle, *Njonja*," he whispered.

"From whom?" she asked.

"From the head of the rebels," he replied.

She invited him inside the house and quickly read the letter. It was appealing to us to contact the United States and ask for help.

The substance of the letter was something like this:

DEAR TUAN OR NJONJA ["Mrs."],

This letter comes to you from a group of us who have rebelled against the government. We are sure of victory, for we have already killed many of their soldiers. So far none of us have lost our lives.

Besides this, we have word that the rebellion is going on in other parts as well. Therefore, we are sure to win. You ought to come into the jungle and hide with us where you will be safe.

We would like to make a request of you. We need help; therefore, we are asking you to call America with your radio and ask them to send arms and ammunition. Tell them to send them by submarine to the coast near Manokwari. We will be hiding and waiting for them.

The messenger was glancing nervously out of the door to see if anyone was coming. Muriel said to him, "We can't do this. Our radio isn't the kind that can send messages a long way. And also we are missionaries. Our business is to preach about Jesus Christ. We can't take part in political affairs. Tell your leader that neither *Tuan* or I can help."

He wasn't satisfied, and he asked, "I've heard *Tuan* preach that we shouldn't kill one another. The rebels want me to take a gun and help them kill people. What should I do?"

Muriel suggested, "Just stay at home, and don't go out in the jungle near them. You don't have to take part in the fighting."

"Oh, I can't stay at home these days. It's too dangerous," he said. "I'll go back and tell them that you can't help, and I'll try to not join in the fighting."

He edged carefully out of the door and made a dash for the shelter of the cocoa trees. Muriel looked at the letter in her hand and uttered a silent prayer. Then she took it to the stove and burned it.

Poor people! They were dreaming of a repetition of World War II, and their dreams were bound to be dashed.

It was a mixture of old memories and old movies. How often I had heard townspeople point to me and say to one another, "He looks like Cary Grant," or "No, he looks like John Wayne."

Once Akwila confided in me, "Do you know what people call you around here? They say you are the American cowboy!"

I guess when it came to the rebellion I must have been a great disappointment to some of them.

When I returned to Manokwari with the summary minutes of our meetings, I didn't feel like marching into the police office with them. I argued with myself that I would save time and long explanations by mailing the report in. This had been done several times before, so I slipped it in an envelope and popped it in the mailbox.

I wasn't to get off that easily, however. Already I had been spotted in town. As I bought a kilo of rice in a Chinese store, I looked up and saw the smiling face and trim fez of Mr. Mutarum, Justice Department attorney.

He approached me pleasantly and said, "I have an order to call you in. Just let me make a phone call, and then we will go to my office."

As he telephoned I wondered what was in the wind. He put it down and said, "You can go ahead of me to my office, and I'll follow in my car."

Shortly after he arrived in his office Captain Sumardjo,

head of the military police, walked in. He looked hard-featured and sullen, and Mutarum sobered up.

"What do you think of the rebellion?" Mr. Sumardjo asked.

I didn't know what he was driving at, but since both men were Muslims I gave the traditional answer they themselves would use if they wished to be noncommittal.

"It is the will of God," I replied.

He fired up: "Do you mean it is the will of God that our soldiers be killed?"

"No, no," I hastened to assure him. "I don't believe that it is His desire. I only meant that it is the permissive will of God. Life and death are under His control."

The captain glared at me, and I knew that I was in hot water. Captain Sumardjo turned to Mr. Mutarum and switched to Javanese which I couldn't understand. But I could tell Mr. Mutarum's reply was, "No, we can't do that. He is a missionary."

The questions continued.

"Do you have any guns?"

"Only a BB rifle belonging to my son."

"What do you know about this insurrection?"

I explained to them briefly what I knew.

"Do you have a radio transmitter in Saowi?"

"Yes sir, all our mission stations have radio transmitters, and it is a safety requirement. We have licenses for each of them."

"You have more than one?"

"There is one in working order at Saowi and three others in the warehouse."

The two men talked again in Javanese. Then Mr. Mutarum said, "Your family will have to move in to

Manokwari. We will send an army truck and a car with you to get your things. You will have about two hours to pack. Do you have a house in town where you can stay?"

I was taken aback. "Do you mean for us to move today?"

"Yes," he replied.

"Well," I answered, thinking quickly, "there is an empty mission house next to our office."

"Good!" he declared. "You can take your scooter there first, and we'll see that you are escorted out to Saowi to pick up your family and belongings."

It was midafternoon when I reached home, accompanied by military police. Muriel looked inquiringly at me. I had missed lunch. Where was my scooter? What were these police for?

"Another exciting adventure in the Lovestrand household," I blithely told her. "We have orders to move to town and are given two hours to pack and take what we can."

After we entered the house, the MP in charge asked, "Where are the transmitters?"

"One is in here," I said, leading him into my study. I turned it on. I tried to call Sentani, "Saowi for Sentani."

It was 3:30 P.M., the regular afternoon scheduled time. No one answered. Then I called Nabire, "Nabire. Nabire. Saowi for Nabire."

The answer came strong and clear, "Saowi, Nabire. Go ahead."

This was the MAF pilot, Dave Peel, and having transported the field council members, he was up-to-date on our local problems.

"Nabire, Saowi station is closing down. They are taking both the radio and me in."

"But why?" queried Nabire.

"I don't know. I guess I must be a bad egg. Saowi over and out."

I detatched the antenna wire and the clamps from the car battery. Then I handed the small package, smaller than a portable typewriter, to the MP. He took it out to the car.

"Where are the other transmitters?" he asked.

"Out in the storehouse," I answered. And out to our storage building we went with two other MPs. I quickly located an old CRMF (Christian Radio Missionary Fellowship) transceiver and began to hunt for the other two sets. At last I uncovered them, old Signal Corps radios. One of our missionaries had brought them out, hoping to use them between two of our stations which were very close together. They only had a range of about ten miles. When we had brought them to MAF to fix, they said we should have thrown them in the sea. Someone left them in the storehouse instead, and I wished right then that we had followed the MAF pilot's advice.

Two hours sped by rapidly, and we could take only the most necessary personal and household effects. Muriel was able to give her sewing machine to one of the teachers' wives. Most of the students were already on their way home, and it was a sad departure from the campus. The work was at a halt, and the future uncertain.

We started out for Manokwari. The truck went first, and our family followed in the police van. It had a Chinese driver, and two MPs got in with us.

The guards at the airfield stopped us, and the MP in charge explained to them that we were being moved to Manokwari. He came over to where we were and pointed out the radios. I heard the soldiers talking to one another, saying, "He's making connections with people outside. Let's throw him out of the country!"

They were in an ugly, menacing mood. One of them was inspecting some BB shot from Tim's air rifle. He came over with the shot in the palm of his hand.

"What have you got here?" he shouted. "Bullets! Bullets to kill us soldiers."

The man in charge of our convoy decided it was time to move on and gave orders to the drivers to start. As we began to roll forward the soldier holding the BB shot raised up his arm and flung it in the window. It splattered in the driver's face.

Muriel looked very solemn as we drove into town. The children were wide-eyed and quiet. Finally she said, "I've never seen such hatred on people's faces. It almost made me cry. Of course, in a way you can't blame those soldiers. They want revenge on anyone they can find that they think has anything to do with the rebellion."

Our two vehicles arrived at the empty mission residence at about six o'clock in the evening. We unloaded our possessions, but the military police beckoned to me to get back in the car. I left Muriel and the children and stepped up into the van. Seated in the back with the Saowi transmitters, I waved the family good-by.

A Family Under Arrest

"*Where are we going?*" *I asked the driver.*

"I am instructed to take you to Mr. Mutarum," he told me. This proved to be more difficult than he thought for the office was closed. But after a stop at the military camp, the driver found out where Mr. Mutarum's home was.

When we got there, Mr. Mutarum was eating his supper. "Oh, yes," he said. "I have some more questions to ask you this evening."

"Would you mind if I went back to have my supper first?" I asked. "I haven't had anything to eat since breakfast."

"Why sure, sure," he agreed, and he told the driver to take me back to the house. There Muriel fixed me a meal, and we had a brief time to pray over our problems. Then I kissed her and the children and left a second time. I was taken to the military camp.

That night the interrogation continued until one o'clock. Mr. Mutarum asked most of the questions, going back over much the same ground as before. Captain Sumardjo sat glowering at me from a corner, and on one occasion when I hesitated on an answer, he interjected sarcastically, "The *Brimob* have ways of making a person talk!"

I felt a wave of resentment rising within me, followed by the realization that this would not do. *Lord, give me grace,* I prayed.

Mr. Mutarum spent a lot of time typing up his record of my statement, but he finally stopped short. He gathered the papers together, pursed his lips and informed me, "You are now under arrest, Mr. Lovestrand."

"Does that mean house arrest?" I asked.

"No, you will not be going back to your family. I think that it is best for you to stay right here. We'll move a bed into this office for you."

"And what next?"

"You and your family will be sent to Djakarta as soon as we can send you there, and then you will be deported."

"Well, if I am sent to Djakarta, will I be able to see a lawyer or the American ambassador there?"

"Yes," he answered. "You will be able to see the ambassador and get a lawyer if you need one. I'll be by in the morning, and you can sign this statement for me."

The next day when he returned he had the papers all ready for my signature.

"Please sign right here," he said.

"Ah, Mr. Mutarum," I demurred, "You mentioned that when I get to Djakarta I will be able to see my ambassador and a lawyer."

"Yes, that's right," he said.

"I've had second thoughts since last night. I believe that as long as I'm going to Djakarta I'll wait to see my American representatives there. I don't want to sign anything now."

"Come on, Mr. Lovestrand," he begged. "Be *sportiev* ('a sport')!"

"Please, if you don't mind, I'll wait until I've had some legal advice."

Mr. Mutarum did not leave in a happy frame of mind, but I felt that his typed statement had some inaccuracies in it and one point which might be misinterpreted.

To my delight Muriel was allowed to visit me three times a day and bring my meals. She was getting the family ready to leave and was able to make one more brief trip out to Saowi for a few more things.

One day when she was sitting in the temporary quarters in Manokwari, more quiet and pensive than the children were used to seeing her, Joan stood up and went over to the record player. "Oh, Mommy," she said, "don't be discouraged. Just listen to this." She put on a recording of the song, "My Father Planned It All," by Wilbur Nelson.

When Mr. Mutarum visited me again and proferred the statement for me to sign, I still refused.

"If I am under arrest, what are the charges against me?" I asked.

He smiled enigmatically and said nothing. Later an MP brought me a document entitled, "Letter of Arrest," and asked me to sign it. I scanned the paper which said I was being arrested and held on charges that had to do with a certain law.

"Please ask Mr. Mutarum what this law is because I am not going to sign something I do not understand," I said.

The government attorney never did offer any explanation, but he did come to tell me that the M. S. *"Sangihe"* was in port and that we would be sailing on it under guard. Knowing how crowded the inter-island steamers usually were, I asked him if our family would have adequate cabin space. He assured me that he would deal directly with the ship captain about this. The last I heard from Mr. Mutarum, he said most graciously to his prisoner, "I hope that I can go and visit you in America some day."

It was a great treat to be allowed to visit the Manokwari missionaries just before leaving. The field council members were all still there because the MAF plane had not been allowed to return. Some of the Bible school students showed up, and as I clasped their hands, the tears came to my eyes.

On board the *"Sangihe"* we were escorted to a small cabin with two bunks. My protest was unavailing, and I was told reprovingly, "This boat is overcrowded, and we had to make someone vacate this cabin so that you would have a place. We told Mr. Mutarum that we didn't have space for you, but he insisted that you go on this ship."

"I'm sorry," I answered, "I didn't know how things were. I only asked for more room because he promised us at least two cabins."

As our ship pulled out from the harbor, we began to settle into our cramped quarters. We decided to sleep two in each berth, one child on the settee and another child on two chairs pulled together.

Joan was ten; Danny, eight; Steve, six; and Joel, two. All of them but Joel had their own Bibles and read them in their private devotions. At home in Saowi we had been accustomed to Bible reading and prayer at breakfast, Bible memory practice at noon, and Bible stories after supper in the evenings.

On board the *"Sangihe"* we didn't keep exactly schedule, but we had plenty of time for Bible reading.

One day as we were sailing along, Steve spoke up. "Listen, Mom and Dad," he said. "See if this psalm doesn't talk about us."

His Bible was turned to Psalm 35, and he proceeded to read us the whole chapter:

> Plead my cause, O LORD, with them that strive with me: fight against them that fight against me. . . . Let them be as chaff before the wind: and let the angel of the LORD chase them. . . . For without cause have they hid for me their net in a pit, which without cause they have digged for my soul. . . . False witnesses did rise up. . . . They rewarded me evil for good . . .

This psalm spoke to me frequently in the following months, and whenever I read it I would think of my six-year-old son, manfully entering into his father's battles.

Leaving Manokwari and knowing that in all probability we might never see it again would have been unbearable if it had not been our assurance as a family that all that was happening was in God's plan for us. Muriel and I had been quoting the verse, I Thessalonians 5:18:

> In every thing give thanks: for this is the will of God in Christ Jesus concerning you.

This had been our theme throughout the summer, and we kept on repeating it aboard the *"Sangihe."*

Muriel brought along Isobel Kuhn's book on the trials of the Matthews family in Communist China, *Green Leaf in Drought Time*, not fully realizing what an identity of spirit we would feel with them before we were done. I had read this account before, but I reread it now. It did much to fortify my heart.

Our ship did not go directly to Djarkarta. Far from it. We seemed to meander slowly here and there, seemingly without purpose. It chose the northern ports of Sulawesi (the Celebes), Balikpapan in Borneo, and back to Makassar in southern Sulawesi.

At first we were not allowed to disembark at any place. But as we became acquainted with our two guards, Welas and Suwardi, they must have decided that we were not too dangerous. One Sunday in port they escorted Muriel and the children to church. Suwardi, who seemed the brighter and carried our papers, professed to be a Christian. Welas, heavyset and slower moving, was an amiable sort. Either he liked children to begin with or ours deliberately set out to steal his heart. They established quite a friendship with this sergeant of the *Brimob*.

At one port we ill-advisedly moved over to a larger cabin on the opposite side of the ship. What we did not know was that the bathroom over on that side did not work. It was next door to our cabin, and being overtaxed, it became a health hazard. Hundreds of students had boarded the ship, and about 1,000 were using facilities designed for seventy passengers. The first thing we knew the slop from the bathroom began leaking through the bulkheads and running over the floor of our cabin.

Since we not only slept but ate in our cabin, this seemed intolerable. It was impossible to move, however, and we just suffered in silence.

We arrived at the port of Surabaja on the eastern end of Java on August 31. Passengers began to disembark at once, but we were told to stay on board. This was our twentieth day on the *"Sangihe,"* and the prospect of another week or so of its slow cruise to Djakarta did not thrill our souls.

Suwardi suggested at last that we get off and go straight to the capital by train. He admitted that he would be glad to leave the ship himself. Since we had no money or passports, he went off to make the necessary arrangements. Our passports had been picked up by the police and never returned to us. As far as money was concerned, West Irian still used a different currency from the rest of Indonesia. Since it was not negotiable elsewhere, we brought none of it along.

A navy jeep came for us and our baggage. At the railroad station Suwardi bought tickets for five seats on the night train, and we were allowed to get on at five o'clock. Welas came along with some sweet rolls he had bought and gave them to the children. Later the guards told us that there was a diner on the train and paid for our meals in it.

Our party numbered eight, and we had only five seats. We were so glad to get off the ship that it didn't matter. The train rumbled on through the night and into the next day, not reaching Djakarta until the afternoon. We sat for an hour in the station there until an inspector of police named Mr. Moedjito came to get us. We piled our whole entourage into his jeep, and he headed for the *Sekkib* or Office of West Irian Affairs.

Again we sat and waited, this time outside the office of Komisaris Hardjanto. Clerks came and went, but we were ignored. Ignored that is by all but one Papuan man who greeted us warmly. He had made a profession of faith some years back in one of our open-air evangelistic meetings in Manokwari.

Mr. Moedjito finally returned and told us, "You will be housed in a place up in the mountains. It is near Tjiloto. I'll take you out to eat before you go."

After a meal at a restaurant, two jeeps came to take us on our way. As we rode along through the streets of Djakarta I saw many familiar sights but not a single foreign face. Secretly I had been wishing that we would meet a missionary who would recognize us, for we had dropped out of circulation completely. No one of our friends knew where we were. It looked as though our whereabouts would remain a mystery, for our cars sped out into the country.

After a while we entered the town of Bogor where the summer palace is located. Less than three months before I had visited here as one of the special delegates to the government conference and heard President Sukarno address us. Now I stopped at Bogor, but at a somewhat less pretentious place, the police station!

Ten minutes later we were off and the jeeps climbed the winding road up the mountain called *Puntjak*. Darkness descended as we crossed the pass and descended to the other side. At Tjipanas we had another brief check with the police and then a delay of an hour. The police chief here was named Rebet Soewarno.

At last our weary family was led to the jeeps again, and we drove the short way to Tjiloto. We entered the driveway of a vacation cottage.

"Here is where you will stay," we were informed.

We went in to look over our quarters. The house had a living room with an imitation fireplace, a combination dining room and kitchen, and three bedrooms.

"You will have only two of these bedrooms," I was told. "The third one will be for your guards."

Harold Lovestrand (center background) shows slides to a group in Manokwari soon after the Lovestrands' arrival in West Irian.

An old man whom Lovestrand met during his first trek into the jungle to find the bodies of the martyrs.

Jerimias Warijo (left), who planned the murder of missionaries Walter Erikson and Ed Tritt, and his accomplices.

Looking down on the grave of Walter Erikson at the spot where his body was found on the bank of the Aifat River in the Bird's Head area of West Irian.

A native hut built in a tree near the place where Erikson and Tritt were slain.

Harold Lovestrand teaches three young men at a short term Bible school held during his first term on the West Irian field.

Part of the Hattam-speaking congregation in Manokwari.

A chapel service at the Erikson-Tritt Bible Institute in Soawi-Manokwari, West Irian.

The first graduates of the Erikson-Tritt Bible Institute. Akwila Baransano (front right) was with Lovestrand the morning of July 28 and was arrested at the airport two hours before the rebels attacked the army post in Arfai.

Harold Lovestrand greets Governor Kaisepo of West Irian at the Bogor Presidential Palace in June, 1965, during the indoctrination lectures for missionaries.

Major General Sutjipto (left), Head of West Irian Affairs, and Dr. Johannes Leimena, then II Deputy Minister to President Sukarno, at the Bogor indoctrination lectures.

President Sukarno and his second wife, Hartini, just after he had addressed the missionaries at the Bogor lectures in June, 1965.

Former Indonesian Defense Minister General Nasution and his family enjoying the Asian Games held in Djakarta in 1962. Sitting on the left is his daughter Erma Siryani who was brutally killed by the rebels of the "September 30 Movement." General Nasution is now Chairman of the People's Consultative Congress. (*Pana photo*)

ndonesian President Sukarno announces a major cabinet reshuffle n Monday evening, February 21, 966, a month before Lovestrand's release. (*Pana photo*)

Former Indonesian Foreign Minister Subandrio sits emotionless facing the rows of six military tribunal judges who sentenced him to death (October 25, 1966) for his part in attempting to overthrow the government in September, 1965 (*Pana photo*)

Students cheer an army tank crew on Madjapahit Avenue near the Presidential Palace in Djakarta following Sukarno's surrender of power to the army in March, 1966. (*Pana photo*)

Indonesian paratroopers guard the Merdeka Palace in Djakarta during the army takeover in March, 1966. (*Pana photo*)

The Lovestrand family. First row, left to right: Steven, Muriel, Joel, Harold, Dan; second row: Joan, Tim, Andrea.

10

Impasse Reached

Three weeks had elapsed since the "Sangihe" steamed out of Manokwari harbor, three long weeks on a crowded freighter crowned with a trip on a crowded train. We were glad of the opportunity for short walks in the Tjiloto hills. Muriel and the children could roam off by themselves, but when I accompanied them, Welas and Suwardi always tagged along.

We had expected that on arrival in Djakarta we would immediately be put in touch with the American Embassy. Instead of getting our questions answered and our case cleared, we had been spirited away to a mountain hideout. Our friends would be waiting for word from us, and we had no means for getting in touch with them.

With no indication how long our enforced vacation in the hills would last, we settled back to enjoy it. Our situation had certainly bettered from shipboard. Meals were brought in from a local restaurant, and we had everything done for us—dishes, cleaning, and laundry. Our only complaint would have been insufficient bedding for the cool nights.

"I know what Paul meant when he said he knew how to be abased and how to abound," Muriel remarked. "This is quite a deluxe jail."

77

"We may as well enjoy it while we can," I said. "I expect I still have an investigation ahead of me, and it is going to take grace and wisdom from the Lord to be a good testimony for Him."

Komisaris Hardjanto and several other men from the *Sekkib* office turned up on September 5. They talked informally with both Muriel and me, and about supper-time they left.

Just as Muriel was getting ready to put the children to bed that evening Welas came to tell us that he had had a telephone message that we would be moving out immediately.

We packed hastily, wondering whether we would be taken back to Djakarta. Only as we drove out on the main road and turned in the other direction did we realize that we were headed for some brand new destination. We were descending to a lower altitude. Near Sukarnagali the car turned off on a dirt road, and we eventually stopped in the grounds of a country villa. This house, unlike the one we had left, had no electricity. A servant brought in a kerosene pressure lamp and some candles, and we began to inspect our new surroundings. We found two large bedrooms, each with two double beds. Muriel and I chose one room with Joan and Joel, while Danny and Steve shared a room with the guards.

The next day we began to explore the grounds. We speculated that we had been moved to this more remote location in order to keep us out of sight of the main road. Our brood of four had been quite conspicuous to passersby in Tjiloto.

There the guards gave me more freedom, and I delighted in this. They didn't bother to follow me when I

took walks with the family, and I appreciate
away from close custody for a change.

Two days of this and a jeep pulled up in the yard. The
man who brought our meals got out, followed by two
policemen. "Mr. Lovestrand, you will come with us,
please," they said.

I picked up my Bible and went along with them. They
volunteered no information as to where they were taking
me, but it turned out to be the first cottage in Tjiloto.

We walked into the living room and sat down. We
conversed there in a desultory way until we heard the
sound of another car coming in the driveway. One of the
guards jumped up. "They're here!" he exclaimed.

I stood up to welcome the newcomers. I recognized
Inspector Moedjito who had met us in Djakarta and
Inspector Rebet Soewarno of the Tjipanas police depart-
ment. The others were a Mr. Sutjipto of Immigration and
Hisom Prasetyo, government prosecutor from the Public
Prosecutor's Department.

We sat down around a table, and Mr. Prasetyo commenced the investigation. "Mr. Lovestrand, we have
been appointed by the government to investigate your
case," he said. "Are you ready to begin?"

"*Bapak,*" ("Father," a term of respect) I addressed him,
"there are many things which I do not understand about
this case. I have not been told why I am being held. No
one has informed me what charges are laid against me. I
have been held without being able to get a lawyer, and I
have been held, a citizen of another country, without
being permitted to see my ambassador. Apparently I am
the one who is the accused, yet my wife and children are
also being held. In Manokwari I was told by Mr. Mutarum of the Public Prosecutor's Department that we

would be deported as soon as we reached Djakarta. He also said there would be no question about my seeing the American ambassador. This has been denied me. With so much that goes against my sense of justice, I am not ready to begin talking to you."

"What? You are not ready to begin?"

"No, *Bapak,* for I do not know what it is all about."

"Don't you know how serious it is to refuse?"

"I know that I am in a serious situation, *Bapak,* but there is so much I do not understand about the government and what it is trying to do to me."

"Are you trying to humiliate the government and us, the officers of the government, by refusing to begin?"

"No, *Bapak.*"

The others joined in with vehemence, "You are not in your own country. You are now in Indonesia!"

"Don't forget that you are responsible to the Indonesian government when you are in Indonesia."

"In America you follow American laws. Here in Indonesia you follow Indonesian laws."

"You'll see the ambassador when we get ready to let you see him!"

This barrage left me nonplussed and all the more confused. When they subsided, Mr. Prasetyo pressed me again, "Now are you ready to begin?"

I shook my head. *"Bapak,"* I said, "I was told that I could see a lawyer and the ambassador in Djakarta, and I think that this promise should be kept. When I see one or the other, I shall be happy to cooperate with you."

The men continued to object and question me, but I would not budge from my position. They turned to one another and discussed the impasse in Javanese. Perhaps I sat there with them for forty-five minutes or so, much of

the time bowing my head and praying, asking God for
guidance. Finally, Mr. Prasetyo brusquely said to the
guards, "Take him back," and I was led away.

Muriel and the children welcomed me and wanted to
know what had happened. There was not too much to
say about my experience. The next day we read, played
with the children and went out for a walk. Two days
later the jeep was back for me.

This time when I was taken to the cottage at Tjiloto,
the investigation was much more formal. The men came
in full-dress uniform, their shoulders bright with stars.
They walked in stiffly and took their seats around the
table as before. They told me to take my seat which I
did. Then I bowed my head and prayed.

When I looked up, the men were looking at me curi-
ously. "All right, Mr. Lovestrand," Mr. Prasetyo addressed me, "we are ready to begin."

I looked around at them all. "*Bapak, bapak,*" I said,
including them all, "two thousand years ago an innocent
Man was brought before His accusers, and He was
pronounced guilty when He had done no crime. I feel
myself under somewhat similar circumstances. I am an
innocent man, guilty of no crime, but I am held like a
criminal without recourse to legal help. I still ask you to
let me see a lawyer or the ambassador. I was promised
this in Manokwari."

They were furious with me. "Are you calling us liars?"
one demanded.

"Don't you know what these uniforms stand for?
These are the uniforms of the Indonesian government.
Are you making fun of the government of Indonesia?
Don't you respect the laws of Indonesia?"

Quietly I answered, "I don't mean to insult either the

government of Indonesia or you gentlemen. But now that you mention it, I was told on several occasions that my family and I would only be here two or three days, and we have been out here over a week. I was told that I would have access to a lawyer and the ambassador, and I have not seen them. One of you told me that our passports were not here from Manokwari, and another said that they were here."

Rebet Soewarno stood up angrily and said, "Listen to him. He is calling us all liars." He started to stamp around the room.

Mr. Moedjito shook a finger at me, his voice climbing in a crescendo, "You are the liar, and we know you are guilty!"

Mr. Soewarno sat down, and Mr. Prasetyo tapped the table with a pencil, "Now, Mr. Lovestrand, are you ready to begin?"

I said nothing.

"First tell me all that you know about the rebellion in Manokwari," he insisted.

I looked at him levelly. "Tell me, Mr. Prasetyo, is this matter of investigation supposed to be voluntary, and is it voluntary if I sign the statements afterward?"

"Yes, yes, of course."

"Then, Sir, I prefer not to answer any questions, for as far as I am concerned it is not voluntary until after I have seen a lawyer or my ambassador."

"Oh, Mr. Lovestrand, come on," he said. "Tell us what you know about the rebellion in Manokwari."

I bowed my head, prayed and remained silent.

Mr. Prasetyo remarked in disgust, "I have never seen such an obstinate, individualistic man in all my life."

I realized that to be individualistic in a pro-

Communist society was a crime in itself. Everyone was supposed to be working together for the good of all.

The men continued to attack me and my attitude, my stubbornness and disrespect. I was a liar. I was guilty. I humiliated the servants of the Indonesian government.

One of them shouted at me, "How do you think we feel when you treat us like dirt? Answer me."

Thus goaded, I replied, "I don't know how you feel, but I feel like a man being attacked from all sides by a bunch of crocodiles."

They exploded at this, "Ha! He is calling us crocodiles. He is saying that we are animals!"

Mr. Soewarno and Mr. Moedjito sprang to their feet and paced around the room. Mr. Prasetyo slammed his fist down on the table, "Animals—animals! That is what he called us."

"No Sir," I objected, quite aghast at this scene, "I did not call you animals. I was only trying to describe how I felt."

They sat down again and tried to make me talk, but I remained silent, praying. I was sorry if they had misunderstood me, but I wondered if they were deliberately looking for something they could pin on me.

Mr. Sutjipto tried to get me started. "Mr. Lovestrand, don't you know that we are trying to help you. The best thing for you to do is just to tell us what you know."

I was silent. They turned to one another and held a conference in Javanese about what they should do. Then Mr. Soewarno rose to his feet. He looked at me with obvious distaste. "OK," he said. "You want justice. We'll show you what justice is. Yes, we'll show you Indonesian justice!"

With that outburst, he strode out of the room. Then

one of the other men impassively remarked, "You will not be going back to your wife and family. You will stay here alone."

They walked out to their car. The ignition started. I heard the roar of the motor, the sound of wheels, and then silence. I was alone, but for my police guards—and the Lord.

11

Only Two or Three
More Days

What kind of a cat-and-mouse game was being played with us? Surely there was more to the way that we were being treated than met the eye. I decided to spend special time in prayer and fasting to seek help from the Lord.

For years I had wanted an opportunity for this sort of a retreat. It had never been too convenient, but now I was alone. It is true that the guards walked in and out of the cottage, but they left me very much to myself.

When I told the man who brought my meals that for a while I only wanted a supply of tea, he was surprised and asked the reason why. I told him that it would help me to pray if I fasted. He went off looking very dubious.

My guards were even more disturbed. They could not believe that I did not want to eat anything. I had thought that they would understand because the Muslims fast. They have a month of fasting called Ramadan. When I mentioned this to them by way of illustration, they replied, "It is not like what you are doing. When we fast, we don't eat or drink all day long, but once it is dark we can eat and drink as much as we like."

"Don't worry," I said. "I'm willing to drink so as not to become dehydrated. It won't hurt me to stop eating for a while. I don't want to eat while I'm praying. When I believe God has heard my petitions, I'll eat again."

As I prayed, I remembered Muriel's circumstances, left alone with the children. I prayed for the Lord to free us, but the chief burden of my soul was that God's Spirit would use us in some way for the salvation and blessing of others.

The Lord gave me opportunities to speak to the guards about Jesus Christ, and one of them begged me for an Indonesian Bible. I gave him my copy, and he promised to read it. I hope that he has kept his promise.

On the evening of the second day of my fast the investigation committee appeared. They called me before them and asked, "Why are you fasting? Is it because you are held here?"

"Yes, partly so," I answered, "but mostly because I am seeking the blessing of God."

They tried to persuade me to stop the fast, but I said, "This is a personal matter. It has to do with my faith. I hope you will try to understand."

They tried to get me to talk about my experiences in West Irian, but I said, "I am waiting to see a lawyer or the ambassador."

Before long they trooped out of the house and went their way.

Apart from these occasional interruptions I had much time for Bible reading and meditation. The paraphrase of Paul's epistles, *Living Letters*,* was my constant companion. Among the passages which seemed apropos to me was II Thessalonians 1:4-6:

> We are happy to tell other churches about your patience and complete faith in God, in spite of all the crushing troubles and hardships you are going through. This is just one example of the fair, just way God does things, for He is using your sufferings to make you ready for His Kingdom, while at the same time He is preparing judgment and punishment for those who are hurting you.

Somehow this helped me to see that we were not actually in the hands of men but in the hands of God. My heart filled with praise to God that He was forcing me to trust Him more than ever before. I praised Him because I believed that he would foil whatever schemes were being devised against us.

The next evening I heard sounds outside. Then Mr. Soewarno appeared at the door. He did not act in his usual self-confident, brisk way. He looked over at me and announced reluctantly, "Mr. Green, the ambassador, is here."

I stepped outside the door and saw several figures approaching through the darkness. Then I heard Mr. Soewarno say, "Mr. Green, this is Mr. Lovestrand."

Dignified and somber, Ambassador Green approached me, stopped and bowed, then extended his hand, saying, "I'm very pleased to meet you."

"I'm very glad to meet you, too, Mr. Ambassador," I replied. Mr. Robert Rich, a vice-consul from the American Embassy, accompanied him, as well as a number of Indonesians.

°Kenneth Taylor, (Wheaton. Ill.: Tyndale House, Publishers, 1962).

There were seven in all, and I invited them into the house. The ambassador began to ask me some questions about my treatment during the past weeks and also about the rebellion in Irian Barat.

"When did you first learn about my arrest?" I asked.

"We have known since August 12, the day after you left Manokwari."

He explained that the embassy was expecting the "*Sangihe*" to arrive in Djakarta August 27 and 28. When it did not make port on those days, the embassy could not get any arrival information from the state shipping line on the grounds that such advice was a military secret. We had been in the area of the capital for thirteen days before the embassy received any official confirmation of our whereabouts.

I asked Mr. Green, "Did I do right in insisting on seeing you?"

He replied, "Of course, you were right. It is a common international courtesy that when a national of another country is arrested he should have access to his ambassador.

"I don't suppose your refusal to answer questions has made them feel too happy. I suggest that you go ahead now and answer the questions to the best of your ability. When they give you statements to sign, be sure that they are correct before you sign them. I understand from Dr. Subandrio of the Foreign Ministry that you are just being held for questioning. No charges have been made against you."

The half-hour visit was soon ended, but the ambassador and Mr. Rich left several paperback books for me to read. They offered me candy, but when I learned that they were going on to see Muriel and the children I suggested that they take it all to them.

"We will do everything we can to see that they get the things they need," Mr. Green added. "Also I shall see that your two children in Manila receive news of you."

That night I was happy in the knowledge that Muriel would have some word of what had happened to me. I knew that God was answering prayer.

The next morning the investigation committee came, obviously expecting to get down to business at last. They had a new member who was introduced to me as Mr. Martono of the Immigration Department. He was overweight but not sluggish. As the questioning proceeded, he took a lead, and I could quickly see that he was the keenest, slipperiest, most cunning man I had met. It didn't take me long to decide that he must be a member of the Central Intelligence Body. If this judgment was mistaken, he at least made sleuthing a hobby or was an avid reader of Ellery Queen.

Because I had seen the ambassador, I cooperated with the committee to the best of my ability. I noticed that the questions were practically the same ones that Mr. Mutarum had asked me in Manokwari.

When we took a break, I looked over the record of questions and answers, the majority of which needed no changing.

I saw some minor mistakes and omissions and asked, "May I write down some of this detail? It isn't complete, and you didn't catch all that I said."

"Sure; go ahead," they agreed, and as I sat writing, they added more questions: "Give a brief sketch of your life—where you went to school—every place you have lived—your experience in the army."

They didn't believe that I graduated from a school of religion. Peering over my shoulder, Mr. Martono laughed huskily, "A school of religion? Is that so?"

"Did you ever contact Guam?" another fellow asked.

"No, of course not," I replied. "From examination of our radio transceivers you can tell that their range is only about five hundred miles."

"After your radios were confiscated were there any other radios working in Manokwari?"

"We had no other mission radios there."

They began to discuss this answer among themselves, and though they were speaking Javanese, I could make out part of what they were saying. They wanted to know how the ambassador could have known about our leaving a day after we sailed. Mr. Soewarno had reported Mr. Green's comment.

My interrogators seemed convinced that the United States must have a super spy and radio system in Indonesia. The Communist press and radio had been constantly hammering away against alleged American meddling in Indonesian affairs. These men's minds had been tainted by these anti-American campaigns to which they were constantly exposed. They had heard of the exploits of the CIA, and now they hoped that they had captured one of its ringleaders.

The fact that I was a missionary with a wife and six children merely gave me a perfect cover. Missionaries were no longer granted impunity from suspicion. In other parts of Asia they were labeled the agents of imperialism. Chinese Communist propaganda, spread widely in Indonesia, proclaimed Robert Morrison, pioneer Protestant missionary to China, one of the worst subversives. This sort of nonsense about a great saint of God, a man who performed the monumental work of translating the Bible into Chinese, was capable of creating suspicion of all present-day missionaries.

When I had completed and signed my statement, Mr. Martono read it over. Then he said to me, "That will be all," and I was excused. The committee had a further session before lunch. When we had eaten, I was told to pack for another move.

"Where will it be this time?" I asked.

"You are going to be taken to Djakarta," they told me.

When the man who delivered meals from the restaurant came back, my guards and I got into his jeep. Instead of turning toward Djakarta, he went to Sukarnagali. "It will give you a few minutes to visit with your family," he said.

My heart leaped. This was an unexpected privilege.

In a short while I was reunited with Muriel and the children. They told me about the ambassador's visit to them, which had been the only event on their social calendar! He had promised to try and get school books to them, but none had come so far. Muriel gave me her Indonesian Bible to replace the one I had given away. I was able to pick up a few other things I needed. Then we had prayer and said good-by once more.

My jeep went back to the Tjiloto cottage where the investigation committee was ready to leave. This time I traveled in a backseat with a guard on either side, while Mr. Martono and Mr. Sutjipto sat with the driver in front.

We climbed the pass and started descending to the Djakarta plain. Almost at the bottom of the long, winding road we passed a large villa among the tea gardens.

Mr. Martono pointed toward the house and asked me, "Do you know Bill Palmer?"

"Well, Sir, I don't know any Palmer out here. I've heard of a Palmer in America, one of America's gold medal golf champions, but that is all."

Mr. Martono chuckled scornfully. I didn't know what he thought was so funny until later when I heard that Bill Palmer was a businessman with a film distribution company. He had many influential friends, but the time came when some of them advised him to leave the country. He had made a hasty exit, thus escaping any difficulties which may have been building up for him in Indonesia.

We stopped on the outskirts of Djakarta. My new house of detention was No. 4, Djalan Tjaka Dua in the suburb of Kebajoran. The committee was content to leave me to sit and meditate there.

I shared a room with my guards in this place. One of them was open and friendly, but the other treated me very seriously. From time to time he would write down a note or two, possibly on my behavior. Once he asked me how to spell a word, and I was glad to be of assistance to him. After all, he probably wanted to rise in the ranks.

He was rather careless about his revolver, leaving it under his pillow on several occasions when he left me alone in the room. I would have liked to hide it just to see what his reaction would have been when he found it missing. I resisted the temptation, however, for I wanted to keep on decent terms with him.

If he left it there on purpose as a decoy, I must have disappointed him. He might have left it unloaded with the hope that I would try to break out to freedom. I wasn't seeking my freedom that way, however.

One morning Komisaris Hardjanto dropped by to see me on his way to his office. Of all the officials I met, he was one of the most polite. He tried to encourage me about my case.

"It will only be two or three more days," he said.

I knew the culture too well to accept this sort of palaver seriously. Many Indonesians consider it a lack of tact to tell you the harsh truth. I think that they would tell a man in a hospital with only a few weeks to live, "You are looking improved. Soon you will be out of here, and we will have a party to celebrate."

I thanked the komisaris for coming to see me. I could see that I was not entirely without sympathizers in official circles.

12

Life Begins at Forty

September 17 was my fortieth birthday. I was allowed to walk around in the garden of the house at Kebajoran, and I gladly did this for exercise. During the day I sat on the porch watching the passing parade of people on the street. They went about their business, paying no attention to me. I longed for some friend or acquaintance to go by, if only for a wave of the hand. They were all strangers, however.

I remember that the meals that day were the usual hotly-spiced Indonesian dishes. I ate heartily and enjoyed myself. As I was finishing my supper, Mr. Sutjipto and Mr. Moedjito appeared.

Mr. Sutjipto seemed to be in particularly good humor, well satisfied with himself and with life. He announced, "As soon as you have finished, pack up your belongings. You are moving to another place tonight."

In my bedroom I quickly gathered together my few possessions. I had a suitcase, a briefcase and my banjo-ukelele. When I brought them out into the living room, Mr. Sutjipto ordered me to open them up, saying, "We want to see what you have there."

I was perplexed by this unusual demand, but I opened them. He made an examination of the contents, waited for me to close the cases, and then told one of the guards, "Take these things out to the jeep."

He beckoned to me to follow, and we started on our journey. It took us downtown into the heart of Djakarta, over a side street or two, past a large school, and up to the doors of a massive, concrete building. We had arrived at No 9, Budi Utomo Street.

The entry was heavily guarded, and when Mr. Moedjito told me to wait there, I sat down and looked at the military police around me. I could tell what division they were in from their blue berets. Over in Manokwari most of the military had worn red, pink, and magenta berets. Besides this, I had seen black, purple and green. I wasn't concerned with the colorful headgear at this point; my suspicions were growing that I had arrived at prison.

My suspicions were confirmed ten minutes later when I was called into the small side office of the C Q (charge of quarters). Mr. Moedjito pushed a paper over to me and said, "Sign this, Mr. Lovestrand."

I took the time to read the document. It was from the Public Prosecutor's Department, an order for my detention on the basis that there was enough evidence to suspect me of crime as covered by Law No. 11/1963.

Also because of the need for investigation and in order that I might not escape or commit further crime the detention was necessary. This order was retroactive to August 7, 1965 although made out on September 13. It stated that this order for detention should be presented to the suspect within twenty four hours.

"This says that I should have received it within twenty four hours of the date, and it is three days late," I objected.

"Never mind. Just sign it," I was told.

I wrote my signature but added above it, "September 17, 1965."

Mr. Moedjito frowned. "What do you think you are doing?" he said, "I know that you are a big liar and guilty."

Once again my belongings were inspected. This time everything was dumped out on a table, and then an MP wrote down a list of all the contents as I repacked. While I was doing this I came across my college diploma. I hadn't realized that I had it with me, for it had been at the bottom of my suitcase.

Now I showed it to Mr. Sutjipto, and he read it for himself, "school of religion." *Would he believe it? Would it help substantiate that I was an honest man?* I couldn't tell.

Mr. Moedjito said, "Take out a change of clothes and your toilet articles. All the rest will be kept for you."

"Please may I have my Bibles," I asked.

"All right," he conceded, and I picked up my English and Indonesian Bibles. When I reached for my copy of *Living Letters,* he protested, "You can't take that."

"This is part of the Bible," I explained, and I showed him the book.

He grudgingly assented to my taking it, and I placed it with the small pile I could take into prison.

Then an MP ordered, "Face the wall and hold up your hands!"

I was frisked for weapons and asked to empty my pockets. Do this. Do that. Come this way. Shadows. Footsteps. The clank of keys. Doors open. Doors shut.

It was a nightmare experience, and yet at one place I stepped out into an open-air corridor that looked up to the stars. In one courtyard a group of about thirty prisoners sat watching television. They all turned and stared at me. I held onto my bundle and hurried after the guard. We passed through another gate. This led into a block with four large cells. We continued walking until we came to another gate. This he unlocked, and we went inside. This block had six small cells in a row. A light glowed dimly in the second cell, and its door was open.

"Go in," the guard ordered.

I entered the cell. A thin grass mat lay on the floor with an overstuffed pillow on top of it. I put my bundle down and looked around. There wasn't much to see.

"This is where you will stay," the guard said. "If there is anything you need, just call me. We are at your service and are here to serve you. Let me show you the bathroom."

He led me around behind the cells, and I looked into the washroom and toilet. A huge rat scampered past. Cockroaches scuttled for cover.

"Thank you very much," I told him, understanding that courtesy was part of the game. He would not be able to do very much for me, but we would keep up the pretense.

The large wooden door of my cell slammed shut, and the key rattled in the door. The guard's steps echoed down the walk, and then all was still.

I looked up at the heavily barred window. The ceiling was concave like the archway in a church. The walls were thick, the floor crumbling partly away.

To be in prison was one thing, but why was I placed in isolation? What had I done to deserve this? A flood of bitter loneliness swept over me. For the first time I felt discouraged about the whole affair.

I turned to my Bible and found comfort in Psalm 142:

> I cried unto the LORD with my voice ... I showed ... him my trouble.... When my spirit was overwhelmed within me, then thou knewest my path.... I am brought very low.... Bring my soul out of prison.

As I thought of other passages which the Lord had been bringing to my attention, I began to feel better. Praying to God for protection on myself and my dear ones, I got ready for sleep.

This presented a problem. I had no mosquito net, and the insects were already buzzing hungrily around me. How could I protect myself from their bloodthirsty attacks?

Sitting down on the mat, I tucked my pajamas legs into my socks, my extra shirt over my head. I lay down and tried to huddle out of reach of the mosquitoes. It was rather suffocating, but I began to doze off from sheer weariness. One of my last waking thoughts was, "Some birthday! Some birthday present!"

From time to time the mosquitoes teased and tortured me. I woke up innumerable times and prayed myself back to sleep. Occasionally I would get a bite that would itch like fire. Not till morning did I realize that the mat on which I had been sleeping harbored bedbugs, and these had joined the mosquitoes in the attack on me during the night.

A guard came in and released me to bathe and use the bathroom at six o'clock. Breakfast came at 7 A.M., dinner at 11:30 A.M., bath again at 3:30 P.M., supper at 4 P.M. It did not take me long to become acquainted with the schedule, or for that matter, with every crack and smudge on the walls of my cell.

I asked the guard if he could do something about my bed and told him what misery I had been in. Somewhat later he brought me a cot and a mosquito net. I rolled up the offending mat with joy and pushed it out between the bars, not envying whoever would use it next.

I was quartered in the *Blok Isolasi* (the isolation block) for especially bad or important prisoners. During the first day my solitary confinement was interrupted by a group of prisoners who came in to dig up dirt and remove it to another part of the prison.

They took turns walking up to my cell to see the American. I think I know now how a monkey must feel at a zoo. Some of them just stared at me. One large brute came up and flexed his muscles at me. They laughed and joked, saying, "He's a bad hombre . . . he's a murderer." I smiled wanly at their humor.

"What are you taking the dirt away for?" I asked.

"To make a badminton court over in our section," one of them replied.

"Here, don't talk to him," the guard shouted.

Evidently I was not a fit member for any type of society. I would have to find my fellowship with God alone.

13

Songs in the Night

It wasn't too long before I learned that there was one other prisoner in my cellblock. I had thought at first that I was the only one, but now I heard the guard talking to someone else in one of the other cells. I caught a glimpse of another man being escorted to the washroom.

"Who is the other prisoner?" I asked a guard.

"Dr. Soumokil," he answered, and that was all I knew.

Soon after this I saw my fellow prisoner clearly for the first time. Dr. Soumokil was let out for a period of exercise. He walked back and forth on the veranda on which the cell doors opened. I peered at him through the small barred window in my cell door. He did not turn his head. He did not dare speak to me, but as he passed by he folded his hands together.

I got the message. Pray! I wondered whether he had heard me singing hymns or if the guard had told him I was a missionary. At any rate I had the consolation that I was near another praying man.

A few days later Dr. Soumokil was out again for exercise. I stationed myself at my small aperture and watched him eagerly. He paced up and down. Then the guard stepped to the back of the compound for a few minutes. Dr. Soumokil kept up his steady march until he reached my door. Stopping momentarily he breathed the two words, "Maranatha—Immanuel!"

I knew for certain now that Dr. Soumokil was a Christian, and I sang in my heart. I had been reading II Corinthians 1:7, "And our hope of you is stedfast, knowing that as ye are partakers of the sufferings, so shall ye be also of the consolation." The Lord was giving me rich consolation, and I thanked Him for it.

In the confines of my two-by-three-yard cell small mercies were to be savored. God had another treat in store for me. The keeper of the jail, Captain Slamet Sentosa, came around to inspect his new prisoner. On his second visit I asked him, "*Bapak,* do you think it would be all right for me to have my banjo-ukulele in my cell . . . and a couple of books which are in my suitcase?"

"I think that can be arranged," he answered. "I'll take care of it."

To my joy the guard brought me the books and my musical instrument. I could play an accompaniment to my singing of hymns, choruses and songs. Just strumming a little for fun and relaxation made the time pass more quickly. What a consolation this was!

After having expended my repertoire of music, I decided that since I had so much leisure, I might as well try to compose a song of my own that would describe my feelings in the prison cell. I recognize that I'm not a singer, composer or accomplished banjo player, but I put all three skills together. I'd like to relate to you what came out as a result.

When I first entered prison, I wondered, "Why? Why does all this have to come on me? Why am I so tempted? Why am I so tried? Why do I feel pressed in?"

I was aware that Communism was responsible for much of my trouble and I wondered how I could shelter and hide from its power. Then I wrote:

Why am I tempted, so troubled, so tried,
Circumstances press me sore?
Where may I shelter, where may I hide?
Satanic hosts against me war.

Where would I find shelter? I already knew the answer. In my prison cell I had experienced a keen sense of God's love and presence enveloping me in a way I had never experienced. His presence overwhelmed and thrilled me.

The heavy iron bars 1¼ inches thick, the thick 18-inch walls of the cell and the towering walls outside, topped with barbed wire, plus all the guards of prison could not keep out the Spirit of God. David's words in Psalm 139:7-10 became more meaningful:

Whither shall I go from thy spirit? Or whither shall I flee from thy presence? If I ascend up into heaven, thou art there: . . . If I take the wings of the morning, and dwell in the uttermost parts of the sea; even there shall thy hand lead me, and thy right hand shall hold me.

Even if I made my bed in hell, God would be there. And in my prison cell God's presence was real. All the powers of earth—even the gates of hell—could not separate me from God's love. Where could I find shelter and hide? I wrote the answer:

In His love, Calvary love,
Safe, secure I rest where none can annoy;
In His love, infinite love,
I find comfort, peace, and joy!

Yes, in the midst of trial I first of all found comfort, then a deep, settled peace, and finally a joy that I could sing about. Then I thought about the whys of suffering, pain, and the bewilderment of other innocent people imprisoned falsely. So I wrote a second verse:

> Why is there suffering, why is there pain?
> The innocent wrongly accused?
> Remember Christ suffered, bearing our shame;
> Why should His saints be excused?

As I sang this and played my accompaniment, I thought of Dr. Soumokil and speculated on what he had gone through. How long had he been imprisoned? From whom was he separated? I hoped that he could hear me sing and be encouraged.

Perhaps he had had doubts like I did. I looked around my prison cell which confined me so securely. Was this a triumph for the devil? No, it could not be, not if I refused to accept it as evidence of his power over me. I wrote another verse:

> Here in my prison cell, two yards by three,
> Walls eighteen inches thick,
> Faithfully, patiently prays this missionary;
> Is this the devil's trick?

I changed the chorus here a little:

> No, it's love, Calvary love;
> Safe, secure I rest where none can annoy.
> In His love, infinite love,
> I find comfort, peace, and joy.

This became my rallying cry. It could bring me out of dejection in a hurry. It fixed my eyes on the Lord, and when I looked at Him, when I considered Jesus, I found I received strength to endure.

The days passed slowly, their monotony relieved by this greatest consolation of all—a keen sense of God's love enveloping me. When I wondered if somehow I had stepped out of His will, I found that I had to put the questions to one side. There was no profit in asking myself if I had made a mistake somewhere. Years before the Lord had impressed Exodus 23:20 on my heart, "Behold, I send an Angel before thee, to keep thee in the way, and to bring thee into the place which I have prepared."

I reminded myself that part of God's love was "keeping me in the way" and I rejected the insinuations of my archenemy, the accuser of the brethren.

I measured my window, about 30 inches wide and 40 inches high, and praised God. Yes, it had bars, 1¼ to 1½ inches thick. The space between was about 3½ inches, just large enough to squeeze a tin cup through. I took this as part of God's plan for me. I had the sure confidence that I was in His hands.

Seeing that His pupil was learning the lesson, the Lord proceeded to give me another one. Had I found solitary confinement hard but not too hard for God? What about something even more shattering?

The prisoners from the next block were occasionally brought into our block to use the bathroom. One morning one of these men came running up to my cell door, his eyes staring with fear. He clutched the bars tightly as he exclaimed, "The government has been overthrown. There are soldiers in all the streets, and now the Communists are in control of Djakarta!"

The guards standing nearby did not attempt to stop

him from telling me this. They themselves were non-plussed by the turn of events. How would it affect them? Which side should they be on?

So, I thought, *they have overthrown the government. We all saw it coming, and now it has happened. Humanly, that means my fate is sealed. If the Communists are in power, they'll give me a rough deal.*

I had known that the Communists were gaining strength in Indonesia. It was common knowledge that the Partai Komunis Indonesia (PKI) was the third largest Communist party in the world. There were three million card-carrying Communists. Some twenty-five million were affiliated with the party through labor unions, youth movements and student federations.

What I did not know was how the Communists had moved to take over the country the night before. I did not know that up in Peking the previous evening Chou En Lai had told a delegation from Indonesia, "Something is going to happen in your country tonight."

In collaboration with the Red Chinese, Dipa Nusantara Aidit, Indonesia's Communist party leader, put into action what he regarded as a perfect plan. He had convinced President Sukarno that the army had formed a junta which was plotting to take over power. Mr. Sukarno flew to the Halim air force base at Tjililitan where the Communists had been training men for six and a half months for a coup d'etat. Dr. Subandrio of the Foreign Ministry had managed to leave the city for a visit to the island of Sumatra. The anti-Communist generals in Djakarta were then the object of what the Communists represented as a counterplot. In the hours of the night six of them were killed, and the city was thrown into confusion.

At 7:15 A.M. that morning, October 1, Lieutenant Colonel Untung, commander of the *Tjakrabirawa* (presidential guard), came on the air to announce that what he called the September 30 Movement had foiled a plot by the Council of Generals. He stated that President Sukarno was safely under protection with General Omar Dhani of the air force. According to Lt. Col. Untung, Djakarta was under his control. He sent a telegram to Dr. Subandrio announcing the success of the revolution.

Blow by blow these news items traveled over the prison grapevine, and all the news was bad from the standpoint of most of us. I was one of about 200 prisoners being detained, and many of us were imprisoned for political reasons. A Communist takeover was not going to help any of us.

I began to pray. I had given myself to much prayer before. Now I prayed more intensely than ever. I thought of Psalm 2 where it says:

The kings of the earth set themselves, and the rulers take counsel together, against the LORD, and against his anointed, saying, Let us break their bands asunder and cast away their cords from us. He that sitteth in the heavens shall laugh; the Lord shall have them in derision.

I thanked the Lord for His sovereignty and power. I told Him again that I believed that I was in His hands and not in the hands of men. "Lord, have a good laugh," I prayed, "and upset the plans of the Communists."

While I was on my knees in my cell, located right at the center of the prison, surrounded by row after row of other prisoners and armed guards, God was working. He was working not just because of my prayers. Unknown to me, thousands of God's people were praying for Harold Lovestrand. And because of my plight their attention had been drawn to the people and country of my adoption. They were praying for Indonesia as never before, individually and in groups.

I was unaware of the extent to which God was using my trial to focus the prayers of His saints on Indonesia, and this came at a time when the future of the country was hanging in the balance. In a sense I was a tool in His hands to help their prayers converge on this land. God's people cried out and asked Him to spare it from the ruthless claws of godless Communism.

14

Turned Tables

Aidit in control! I could remember reading a book of his in which he wrote that the workers in the United States "do not possess anything except their working energy which they rent (or sell) to the capitalists so that they will not starve to death."

This book was part of the Communist propaganda which had been given to us missionaries at the conference sponsored by the Office of West Irian Affairs. That was only four months before. The Communist speeches we had heard then didn't sound so funny now. It looked as though the Communist leadership had gained its chance to remake the nation in the image of Red China. That is, unless God intervened.

God already was beginning to intervene. He was already commencing to answer prayer. The very night of the coup, though I did not know it, Muriel and the children were in the city. They had been moved back to Djakarta, staying for a while in the same house I had occupied in the suburb of Kebajoran. The embassy had succeeded in securing their release. They had been placed in the custody of the American authorities who arranged to house them at the Protestant Guest Home in the city.

The Communist plan called for the capture or killing

of eight key anti-Communist generals. The order was
given at four o'clock in the morning, October 1, and
Communist forces immediately moved to seize the military leaders who stood in their way. Muriel woke to
gunfire across the street. What was happening? Cars
raced up and down the street.

More shots rang out at the house of Dr. Leimena, a
prominent anti-Communist who lived across the way. A
little way down the block the Communists burst into the
house of the Defense Minister, General Nasution. Fore-
warned by their gunfire, he leaped out of bed, escaped
through a rear window and fled. Exasperated at not finding him, one of the gunmen shot his little daughter and
left her dying.

The commander of the Army Strategic Reserve, General Suharto, was missed because he had gone to spend
the night in a hospital beside an ill daughter. He returned home after the killers had come for him. Warned
of the plot, he rushed out.

Hurrying to his headquarters, General Suharto began
organizing a counterattack against the Reds. He assumed that the military leaders over him had been wiped
out, and they all had, except for General Nasution. The
other six had been cruelly murdered, some of them after
public humiliation and torture. He stepped into the gap
and gave orders to the army to move in on the Communist forces.

Three days later the same prisoner who had told me
about the Communist take-over returned to my cell with
a delighted smile on his face. "The Communists are on
the run, and the army has control of the city!" he said.

Ah, we could breathe easier. How I rejoiced! How I
praised God for His interfering with the evil designs of

the Communists. He had spoiled their perfect plan. Rumors flew around the prison, and the news was so exciting that it penetrated even to me in the isolation block.

The Communists had lost the initiative, and the end result of their rebellion was in question. This immediately began to influence my relationships with such few people as I had contact with. Those who had previously been afraid of the American "imperialist" were willing to slip me an Indonesian newspaper. Sometimes the guard failed to lock my cell. I was able to go over and talk with Dr. Soumokil about the events of the day, and the news was all encouraging.

Within two weeks Communists began to pour into jail. One evening when Dr. Soumokil and I were in our cells, we heard the lock of the door to our block turn. In came two MPs with another prisoner. They deposited their charge in the cell next to Dr. Soumokil and left. When a few minutes had passed, Dr. Soumokil asked the new arrival, "Who are you? What are you doing here?"

I heard a voice answer, "My name is Sudewa. I'm a schoolteacher from Surabaja, and I'm here because I complained about the government."

"Yes? What were you complaining about?"

"Well, I only have a wage of 19,000 rupiahs a month, and I have a wife and six children. You know that rice costs 1,500 rupiahs a kilogram. It isn't enough for us to live on, and my children are hungry. Someone heard me complaining against the government, and that is why I am here."

"What religion are you?" asked Dr. Soumokil.

"I'm Protestant. My father is a preacher in the Protestant church."

"You ought to know that God can handle your problem then," Dr. Soumokil said. "You'd better pray to God and ask His help."

Prison intelligence performed excellently, and the system had the new prisoner spotted within two days. By then we knew that his real name was Sungkowo, that he was not a teacher or a Christian and that he had been a lieutenant in the intelligence department of the military police. He had been in a fairly influential position in the Communist ranks due to his ability as a rabble-rouser. Our prison intelligence service claimed that he obtained falsified and counterfeit documents which he circulated to the army, navy, and air force intelligence departments. This was aimed at confusing military intelligence and making conditions ripe for the coup d'etat.

When we confronted him with what we knew, he denied it. We insisted that he admit to his true identity and told him more of what we knew. Gradually he admitted to the role he had played in the foiled plot.

About three days later two more lieutenants arrived in the isolation block. When Mr. Sungkowo met them on his way to the bathroom, he extended his hand. They refused to shake hands with their former comrade.

I learned that these three Communists were the officers who seized the government radio station in Djakarta. They were present when Lt. Col. Untung gave his victory speech, announcing the new "government of the people" which had replaced the old government.

The two newcomers blamed Mr. Sungkowo for their capture, feeling sure that he had squealed on them under pressure. During the time they were there together, they would have nothing to do with him.

One day I saw the guards bring in a table, a large light and a tape recorder, placing these by the last cell in the row. Then they told me that I was going to be moved to another section of the prison. Obviously someone important was going to be brought into the isolation block for interrogation. Prison rumor had it that Lt. Col. Untung had been captured and that he was being brought to our prison.

Dr. Soumokil was transferred at the same time that I was. It was a very fortunate move for me, for I was taken to a cell about five times as large as my former one. I was given more freedom, and I was next to a shower room. Moreover, the toilet facilities afforded more privacy than in the isolation block.

That first night I sat up until nine-thirty talking with the other inmates. We squatted by the fishpool in our courtyard and discussed the topsy-turvy spin of events. Here the very man who had proclaimed the victory of Communism was probably sitting in the isolation block I had so recently vacated. It sent the blood coursing through my veins.

A man turned to me and said, "We were so glad when we first heard that you were in prison."

"What!" I exclaimed. "Why would you be glad to have me in prison?"

"Because we knew that you are a servant of God, and we said to one another, 'When the government starts meddling with God's servants, something is bound to happen.' And you see how much has happened."

I was amazed to hear this from a Muslim, but I did not doubt that the leaders like Lt. Col. Untung who had been toppled had stored up judgment for themselves.

Many of the men with whom I associated at this time were political prisoners. They had every reason to believe that hopes were brighter for their release. What a fantastic collection of brains and talent they were, put out of circulation because they could not conform to Communist ideology!

During meals or standing in line for baths, I became acquainted with a number of them. There was Colonel Nikolas Simbolon, former leader of the independence movement in Sumatra. He was a Christian and leader of the Protestant services in the prison. Sultan Hamid Alkadrie, a man in his mid 50's, had said to me, "Just call me Max." He was a former major general and ex-adjutant to the queen of Holland. He very kindly found a pail for me.

Anak Agung Gde Agung was an ex-minister of Home Affairs and former U. N. representative. Mr. Subardjo was the former ambassador to France. Mohammed Rum had signed the document of independence with the Dutch. Mochtar Lubis was the former publisher of a daily newspaper, *Merdeka*. He was an internationally known journalist who wrote too critically of the regime.

Sjafruddin Prawiranegara had been president of the country for a brief time while Sukarno was abducted. A former prime minister and minister of finance who later opposed President Sukarno now was rewarded with a prison cell.

Burhanuddin Harahap was another ex-prime minister; Mr. Sumarsono, the head of a youth movement which had been banned, also was in our company.

Some of these men were in a position to buy what they wanted to make prison life a bit more comfortable. They treated me with chicken dinners, lunches, cookies, razor blades and other amenities. I appreciated their friendliness as much as the gifts which they shared with me.

Not all were financially well off. I was introduced to a

fellow nicknamed "President" Untung, not to be confused with Lt. Col. Untung. The "President" welcomed the chance to tell me his story.

"In the spring of 1963 President Sukarno gave a speech in Bandung," he said. "In this speech he stated that if there was anyone in Indonesia who could guarantee a workable socialistic state, he would gladly surrender the presidency to him. I immediately began to formulate my ideas of how this could be done. Then shortly after, I went to the palace and presented my letter. In it I promised that within ten years we would have a workable, socialist Indonesia if my leadership were followed.

"My letter was taken, and I returned home. About a month later I was called to a government office and interviewed. Another month passed and then police came to my home. I was taken away for an interrogation and allowed to return home. Not many days afterward the police came for me again and said that I was wanted for another interrogation. Instead of that, I was brought to prison. I didn't even get a chance to say good-by to my family. I was arrested on the same charge as you, *Tuan,* subversion. That was almost two years ago, and my case has not come up for trial yet."

Poor "President" Untung! He was a school inspector from central Java with high ambitions but apparently a little naïve. I hope that by this time he has been freed and has been allowed to go back to his work in the schools.

A great many changes for the better are taking place, and surely it would help the country if some of these men were released. They looked at me as a token of good things to come, a harbinger of change. By the grace of God, the tables did turn.

15

A Dirty Business

Six days after our move to more spacious quarters, Dr. Soumokil and I were ordered back to the isolation block. This would have been depressing except that the two of us were given considerably more liberty on our return and also had formed a fast friendship. It was almost like returning back home to be in the familiar cellblock once more.

The former army guards had been withdrawn from the prison, and military police were in charge. Where we had always had two guards watching us, now no one was specifically guarding us. Dr. Soumokil's door was left open all the time, and I was free for hours at a time. The other cells were filled with Communists who were kept locked in their cells except for meals and bathing.

At first I had thought that Dr. Soumokil was a medical doctor, but I now know that he was a Doctor of Laws from Leiden University in Holland. He could speak fluent Dutch, German, English, French, Javanese, Indonesian, and one or two languages of the Molucca Islands.

Son of an Ambonese postal officer and a Javanese mother, Dr. Soumokil received his education during the Dutch colonial administration of Indonesia. After graduation he quickly rose in the ranks until he was head of the Public Prosecutor's Department in Surabaja, the second largest city in the nation. During World War II he was imprisoned by the Japanese in Singapore and then Bangkok. Following the war, he helped. try Japanese war criminals at Morotai, north of Halmahera Island. He also served as minister of public prosecution for East Indonesia. What led then to his downfall?

While serving in the Moluccas, he led the independence movement there. He was chosen president when they declared themselves independent from the rest of Indonesia in April, 1951. The revolution failed, and for thirteen years Dr. Soumokil hid in the jungle, directing sporadic warfare from there against the Indonesian forces. Eventually he was captured and imprisoned.

Many years ago he predicted that Indonesia was going Communistic. It was for this reason that he led a movement against the central government. From his point of view, he always had been one of the leaders in the struggle against Communism in Indonesia.

One day he asked me if he might borrow my banjo-ukulele. He had been a member of a band while in college, and now he performed a one-man concert for me. It was refreshing to hear him play some of the Ambonese melodies, which are akin to the songs of Hawaii. I could close my eyes and picture the strand of Waikiki as he played and sang. But when he stopped, I looked up. Seeing the sixteen-foot walls topped with another four feet of barbed wire, I was jolted back to reality.

This was prison with its routine, a routine which had been broken somewhat by the events of the last weeks but was still much the same.

When I was kept in isolation, I had had long periods

of Bible reading, first in my King James Bible and then in *Living Letters,* my own sessions of exercise in my cell, times for writing, for prayer, and for the regular eating and bathing breaks. Between times and almost always at night I would strum on my banjo-uke. By seven-thirty in the evening I usually became tired of battling mosquitoes and would shelter under my mosquito net. There I could still play and sing.

With the Communists sharing our cellblock, my schedule changed. I took somewhat less time in personal reading and prayer in order to witness and pray with the Communists. All the cells were filled, and sometimes there were two in a cell.

Of all these men there was not one who was not happy to have me pray with him. These were men who had believed the propaganda of Communism and had followed it. Now it had failed, and they had failed. They despaired of their lives and were groping for some kind of security. I was glad to speak with them about the destiny of their souls, and several prayed with me to commit their lives to Christ. I am not satisfied, however, that the results were 100 percent successful.

Take Mr. Sungkowo, for example. He borrowed my Indonesian Bible. He begged, even demanded, that I pray with him, but I always had an uneasy feeling about the sincerity of his intentions.

He seemed to get no comfort from the Lord, though he professed that everything between him and the Lord was right and settled. He said that he received comfort from reading God's Word and from praying, but there seemed to be little evidence of any peace.

Perhaps it was the effect of prison and interrogations, perhaps it was a sense of guilt, knowing that he had been caught and the seriousness of the charges against him. After several weeks his eyes seemed to have a distant look. When he was let out of his cell for his meals or for bathing, he would pace back and forth like a caged tiger.

At one time Mr. Sungkowo told me, "I have been having visions, and God has been talking to me."

Nevertheless, the look on his face did not correspond to what I would call peaceful communion between a Christian and his God. No, it was rather the ghastly, haggard look of a man estranged from his Creator. Nonetheless, there were others who gave evidence of new life in Christ.

One night a new man was brought into our isolation block, and for two days all of us were kept in as much as possible and not allowed to mix. The information quickly spread, however, that this was Mr. Njoto, a brilliant, dedicated young Communist, rated second in importance after Mr. Aidit, the party boss. He was taken out repeatedly for interrogations up front, and the word was that he talked circles around his interrogators. Finally, he disappeared for good.

Other inmates of our block included a navy officer who had traveled much in Communist countries, a major who alledgedly distributed army weapons to Communists, a black marketeer whose chief interest seemed to have been making a few rupiahs by selling stolen goods. We also had Mr. Njoto's brother-in-law and his chauffeur.

In the adjoining block were two bankers who had bought arms from Communist China and distributed them to Communists in preparation for the uprising. I also became acquainted with General Sitobuh, the former governor of North Sumatra. He was accused of embezzling millions of the government's rupiahs to promote the uprising. General Sitobuh borrowed my Indonesian Bible for a week or so.

A corporal from the *Tjakrabirawa* (presidential guard) was shoved into the cell next to mine. I noticed that he was shaking with fear and that he looked furtively about at the rest of us. Rumor had it that he had taken an active part in the October rebellion and that he was suspected of killing someone of importance.

Some days later, I went over to him and asked why he was imprisoned. Corp. Supardi looked frightened.

He didn't give me a direct reply but said, "Now, *Tuan,* I'm only a small man, a corporal, and my superior officers gave me orders. I carried them out, but what was I to do?"

One day I was reading lying on my cot, when I heard, *Rat-a-tat-tat.*

A distant scream rent the air: "Ow-w-w-w-w, Pa-a-a-a-a."

Rat-a-tat-tat.

Silence.

I called over to Corp. Supardi, "Did you hear that?"

He answered in a trembling voice, "Y-y-y-e-ss."

A week or so later I heard more shooting.

Bang! Bang! Bang! Bang!

"Ahhhhhhhhh."

Then, four seconds later, a single solitary shot, *Bang!*

"Did you hear that, Pardi?" I called.

This time Corp. Supardi was apparently sleeping. Maybe that was a blessing.

The prison grapevine carried a conversation heard

reportedly in the front office. It went something like this:

"We've been given strict orders to shoot to kill any Communists who try to escape," said one MP.

"Is that right?" queried another.

"Yes," continued the first, "and we've also been ordered to make it easy to allow certain ones to escape."

"I suppose they don't get very far," ventured the second MP.

"No, but I don't like it," was the answer. "It's a dirty business."

One wealthy Chinese businessman who was in custody did make a break for freedom. He had been allowed to wander down and sit near the main gate, waiting for his meals to be brought in from home. He always offered the guards some of the tasty Chinese dishes he received.

At noon one day he dashed out the gate and down the street. The guards were afraid to shoot after him because children were just leaving school. "Communist—Communist," the guards shouted and the children surrounded him and held him tight.

When he was carried back into prison, his mind broke completely. He would cradle his pillow like a baby and sing it lullabies. Because he was in the cellblock next to mine, I got the full benefit of his screams when he switched to a violent mood. His hopeless, maniac shouts spread a pall over the other prisoners.

There is much about prison life that tends to degrade those who are caught up in it, whether jailors or prisoners. On at least three occasions, I was approached with offers to get a letter out to my wife. Of course it would involve a bribe, a small sum, but delivery was guaranteed. Though I would have liked to get a message to Muriel, I couldn't bring myself to do this. Each time I politely refused the offers. I said, "I can just wait awhile."

They would go away wondering, and I would go on trusting God to provide communication with my wife in some better way.

16

Patience' Reward

The American Embassy inquired of Sekkib when next they might have access to me only to be told by Komisaris Hardjanto, "No more visits are permitted. Dr. Subandrio gave permission for one visit, and Ambassador Green has had that. There will be no further visits."

The embassy kept pressing the Office of West Irian Affairs for its rights to see any American citizen in trouble, and they received assurance that something would be done. On September 27 they received a clarification to the effect that American representatives would be permitted to see me once a week. Two days later they were informed that the former agreement was canceled. Permission to visit me would be limited to once every two weeks. Actually it didn't work out on any predictable schedule at all.

The evening of September 27 I was brought to the *Sekkib* office under heavy guard for my second contact with Ambassador Green. The next week the city was in turmoil because of the attempted revolution. Thus it did not surprise me when the weekly visit from the embassy did not materialize. At the end of two weeks I still had no further contact with them. Then my patience was rewarded. The morning of October 12 an MP came to

my cell with the news, "*Tuan,* here is an envelope for
you. Sign this slip that you have received it, and you may
have it."

It was a communication from the American Embassy.

"*Terima kasih* (thank you)!" I said, signing the receipt
and reaching for the envelope.

Tearing it open, I found soap, mosquito repellant, a
small amount of writing paper, and a letter from Muriel.
She had written October 9, expecting that her letter
would be brought to me in person by someone on the
embassy staff.

Eagerly I read the news about her freedom in the city
and the arrangements made for her housing, how the
three older children were now in the International
School, how Joel, our youngest, was settling down. Joan,
Dan and Steve had classmates from many nations. They
had had some difficulty starting school late, but they
were thrilled to be back with other children again.

The news that Muriel and the children had been
released was announced over the Far East Broadcasting
Company's station in the Philippines the day after it
happened. Friends at home were writing to Muriel, and
she was encouraged by the volume of prayer for me.

This letter and others like it were treasure to be
examined and reexamined. I shared parts with Dr.
Soumokil in order to have someone with whom to discuss
my family news.

She wrote:

I feel guilty when we eat, thinking of what your
circumstances are, and yet I am glad for the children's
sake ... I am so glad that they are at school ... not only

does it keep them up on their lessons, but it fills their days and their thoughts and keeps them from thinking about the problem.

It seems that for me the Lord is gradually removing the drought - first our release, then school for the children, and letters from the children in Manila and our folks, then this house to live in ... but for you the drought has been steadily increasing ... may your leaf be kept green!

I think that I will always be more understanding of widows and their problems. Of course, I have been alone with the children before, but this time it is in a strange community. The missionaries have been so helpful about taking the children to school, and this is one thing that has reminded me to be more helpful to others in the future.

After reading Muriel's letters my heart would be full. She would say, "We can meet at the throne," and how well I knew this. It was as though we had never been separated in spirit. We were going through this experience together, and countless Christian friends also were reaching out to us by prayer, joining us in a stand of faith and praise to almighty God.

The banjo-ukulele helped me express my confidence as I sang other verses to my prison song:

> In a strange city, a mother of six
> Gathers four around her knee;
> Her husband, a preacher of righteousness,
> Is barred from his family.
>
> Is this love? Yes, God's love,
> Safe, secure, they rest where none can annoy;
> In His love, infinite love,
> There is comfort, peace, and joy!

And for my son and daughter in high school over in Manila there was this:

> Up in Manila, two M.K.'s at school
> Wonder why Dad's in jail;
> I'm a prisoner of love, my daughter and son,
> Of God's love that can never fail.
>
> In His love, I'm a prisoner of love;
> Safe, secure, I rest where none can annoy.
> In His love, infinite love,
> I find comfort, peace, and joy!

I thought back to my years at Bob Jones University and that memorable day when I found myself sitting beside a striking girl student in the dining hall. The effect of this meeting had been stimulating, ecstatic, ethereal! After several insufferable days of waiting, courage defeated timidity, and I had asked Muriel Lang for a date. When she accepted, I took two of my college roommates off campus for a steak supper celebration.

On that first date we learned that our backgrounds were almost perfectly matched. Both of us came from large families; both of our fathers were carpenters by trade and were born in Scandanavia; both mothers were American born but of Scandanavian descent. Both of us had been born in the same month of the same year. We had both received Christ as Lord and Master, and we wanted to serve Him at His direction.

That was the commencement of a friendship which developed into an intimate fellowship. We were married between our junior and senior years of college, the summer of 1948. The next summer we had our first child.

That fall of 1949 I moved my family to a one-room

apartment in the cement jungles of Chicago where for two terms I attended Moody Bible Institute. Muriel and I were accepted as candidates under The Evangelical Alliance Mission in the spring of 1950 with the proviso that we attend the missionary candidate school sponsored by the mission. That summer we took part in the candidate school, after which we were ready to visit churches in behalf of our call to Indonesia.

Now after seventeen years of married life Muriel and I were still sharing a vital partnership, even if we were sharing separation. I suppose most people who enter prison crave companionship, those contacts for which the heart hungers and from which it is deprived.

Muriel's letters supplied much of this. They expressed what I needed to hear, and they sounded so much like her. It was as though the words echoed in my ears:

Since in our married life we have had mostly joy and so little sorrow or suffering, I guess God sees this is what we need. Especially if we are to be used in the way we long to be. Remember your "suffering" sermon on furlough? Maybe the Lord gave you that, not only for your hearers, but for your benefit as well.

And when Thanksgiving came:

I told the children that we would make some kind of poster or table display, showing things we are thankful for. First on my list would be you—though it is difficult to write all that being your wife has meant to me—yet I consider it blessing No. 1.

I thanked the Lord for Muriel. He was the source of our blessing, and while I yearned for my wife and children, He satisfied the emptiness of my heart. I found that God had new dimensions for my fellowship with Him. I was being brought into a new comprehension of communion with Christ.

Dr. Soumokil wanted to be encouraging when he said, "Don't you forget, Mr. Lovestrand, that you are a citizen of the world's most powerful nation. Your country will not let you down. You won't be kept here long."

"My country is great, but it has its limitations in trying to extract me from this predicament," I replied. "I appreciate all the embassy is doing for me, but it is not enough. God is going to have to help me, too."

A Pawn in the Game

"Mr. Lovestrand, you were responsible for reporting that the school boys left, and you should have used your radio to report the bridge." Mr. Martono fired the accusation at me during a second interrogation session.

He pressed me to confess my guilt for these failures. I wasn't feeling very well, and being under duress, I gave him what he wanted. It certainly wasn't my confession. It was Mr. Martono's, for he wrote it out the way he wanted it.

Once I said, "I feel—"

He snapped back, "It can't be 'I feel.'"

When I qualified one statement with "perhaps," he ruled that out.

"You may not say, 'perhaps'!"

When I said, *"Saja mengaku bahwa saja tidak laporkan,"* which means, "I confess that I did not report," he corrected this to read, "I confess that I am guilty of not reporting."

I didn't try to defend myself, but I was thinking that those twenty-five schoolboys running because they were scared stiff didn't sound very important at a time when probably 2,500 to 3,000 fled from Manokwari. I estimate that at least 1,500 mountain people went back to the mountains and probably 1,000 coastal people left for Biak, Numfor, Wandamen and Sorong. Many of them must have gone without a travel permit.

As far as the radio transceiver was concerned, I didn't think of using it. I supposed that the government would rather not have the news broadcast all over, for anyone with an ordinary portable radio could pick up our frequency. People often did listen in to our mission broadcasting.

After the interrogations, I would sometimes wake up in my cell and wonder when this dream would end. It seemed so fantastic for me to be in prison. Then verses in the Epistles would come to my mind. The *Living Letters* paraphrase of I Peter was such an encouragement:

> "Suffering is all part of the work God has given you. . . . When your body suffers, sin loses its power, and you won't be spending the rest of your life chasing after evil desires . . . Let Him have all your worries and cares, for He is always thinking about you and watching everything that concerns you" (I Peter 2:21; 4:1-2; 5:7).

I could see that I had a God-given work to do there in captivity, and also that He always had me in His thoughts.

Just after dinner, on the afternoon of October 15, I was called by an MP who told me to hurry and dress. I was wanted at *Sekkib*, the Office of West Irian Affairs. Since it was a hot day, I bathed quickly. I dressed and then left the prison under escort.

Outside on the streets cloth banners stretched across the road in many places. I had noticed these banners before but had not bothered to read them. Now I noticed that one of them read, "Crush the CIA." Another declared, "Crush Imperialism and Capitalism." Passing the U.S. Embassy, I saw that there were similar banners outside its gates.

The *Sekkib* building also had these public slogans denouncing the United States. The military police brought me inside. It was practically empty because it was a Friday afternoon, the Muslim day of worship.

Mr. Martono met me and motioned for me to sit down. Silence ensued until he asked me, "What do you think of the present situation?"

"Well," I answered, "you know that the Chinese Communists have been preaching the violent overthrow of governments, and now you see the result."

Then an American entered the room. It was Dale Diefenbach from the embassy, and I realized that this was one of the promised contacts with American representatives. Mr. Diefenbach brought me a few toilet articles and some items of food. He also had a letter from the ambassador and a *Newsweek* magazine containing a report on the abortive coup d'etat.

"I thought you might be interested in reading about what happened," Dale said.

"I would be interested in reading all about it," I answered, "but you'd better take the magazine back, Dale. They won't let me have it anyway. None of the other reading matter the ambassador gave me has been forwarded to me yet."

The letter from the ambassador which was lying on the table in front of us disappeared into someone's pocket. It had to be censored before I could be allowed to read it.

Dale asked how I felt, and I told him that I hadn't

been feeling too well. Physically, I was beginning to feel tired and worn out. I had pain under my arm, under the lower ribs on each side, and in the groin. I attributed this to the parasites that I had picked up in West Irian, mainly filariasis.

Then I started to tell him how poorly I felt during interrogation, but Mr. Martono didn't want him to hear anything about that. He broke in, "Well, that's enough now. I think that you have visited long enough."

Dale promised to get some medicine for me. We waved good-by, and one more visit with the outside world was over.

On my return to the isolation block, my fellow prisoners were curious to know how things were going. I mentioned that I had seen many anti-American and anti-CIA banners.

One of the prisoners said, "I know exactly why those banners were there. Do you know what I saw in the papers before you came to prison? One of the Djakarta newspapers had huge headlines which said, "*Kedok CIA Ditjabut.*" (The mask of the CIA has been pulled off). Then in smaller letters it said that an agent of the CIA had been captured and was being sent to Djakarta for questioning. Do you know who that agent is?"

"No," I said in all innocence. "Who is it?"

"You," he exclaimed. "I'm sure of it. Look, were you ever in the military service?"

"Yes," I answered, "I was in the signal corps for awhile."

"Ah, just being in military service was enough to put the finger of suspicion on you, but being in the signal corps makes it worse."

"I know," I replied. "They accuse me of being an

expert radio technician, but I was only a teletypist and clerk."

"There you are! Can you think of anything else that might cause suspicion to fall on you?"

"Well, I did have a mission-owned radio sender in my house for communication with the interior stations. And I have a private pilot's license."

"Wow! You really are loaded."

With that we broke up our little meeting and went our separate ways, but from the newspapers which found their way into prison, from the interrogations, and from one or two other sources, I found out that I was suspected of being an agent of the CIA, an expert radio technician engaged in sending messages out of the country, an agent who was financing and instructing the rebels of Manokwari, and a smuggler of Israeli arms into West Irian.

Of course, none of these suspicions were true, but I am sure that to my fellow prisoners they added some glamour to my presence in their midst.

Speaking to Dr. Soumokil about these charges, I said, "Do you know, they say that I was sending messages to Guam, two thousand miles away, and our set could only reach about five hundred miles. It was registered and licensed by the government. It is a set with crystal frequencies and pretuned. Anyone with a shortwave radio could pick up our conversations.

"And do you know, I don't have any money to do any financing. I can tell you this though, if I had been instructing those rebels as I'm accused of doing, they would have done a much better job than they did. They were sloppy, untrained and unorganized. They missed lots of opportunities to cripple and eliminate their foes."

"Oh," said Dr. Soumokil, for thirteen years a guerilla fighter in Ceram, "what would you have done?"

"Now, I am a missionary. My work is preaching the gospel and winning people to Christ. I could never imagine forsaking the job the Lord has given me to get involved in politics or guerilla fighting."

"Yes, but what would you have done?" he persisted.

"Well, it was obvious the rebels lacked good organization. Second, they lacked planning and strategy. Third, they needed a simple but effective reconnaissance and intelligence system.

"Communications and supply would have to be disrupted. I think it would have been simple to destroy the power plant in Manokwari merely by rolling the drums of diesel fuel into the building and using a match. The same would be true with the powerful radio station at the airport. There was plenty of aviation gasoline nearby.

"Then the army convoys were traveling too fast. I know of blind turns where a simple large cable strung at the right height across the road would cause a disastrous situation. An ambush at the time of impact would have been most effective.

"It was obvious that many soldiers who guarded the airstrip were sleeping during the day in one of the buildings. Two well-placed grenades would have finished them. When the patrols made treks into the jungle, this would have been one of the most opportune times for the rebels who knew all the trails. Then in the town they could have struck terror in the hearts of everybody by night attacks, explosions and fire."

Dr. Soumokil was listening to me intently.

"But, Soumokil, I couldn't do it," I said. "My job is preaching the gospel of Christ."

Dr. Soumokil chuckled and said, "Well, if God called you to do it, you could. You know, I would have liked to have had a man like you in Ceram."

Now wasn't that some way for a preacher and a doctor of laws to talk! Yes, maybe prison does affect a person.

One of the prisoners had a much more realistic view of the CIA than the local newspapers or his fellow inmates. "I know that you aren't an agent of the CIA," he sniffed. "The best agents of the CIA are not foreigners. They are Indonesians."

"Why am I being held then?" I asked.

"You are useful for propaganda purposes. The common people do not think very deeply about these things, and they are easily fooled, Someone is holding you like a trump card, waiting to be played."

18

White Magic

Dr. Soumokil, for all of his western education, had his roots deeply in Indonesian culture. One day he fell to discussing magic with me.

"Of course, there is black magic and white magic," he said.

"Oh? What is the difference?" I asked.

He looked at me with amazement at my ignorance. "Why, black magic is for bad purposes like killing people," he replied, "but white magic is always for a good purpose. I have an uncle who is a sorcerer, but he always uses his powers for good purposes."

Intrigued, I asked, "What did he do?"

Dr. Soumokil was only too ready to regale me with the exploits of his uncle. "When I was Minister of Public Prosecution, we had a Japanese ship come into port. I was warned that it had smuggled goods aboard, but no matter how much our men searched, they could find nothing.

"I went to my uncle and asked him if he would help me, and he said, 'I'll help you.' We went down to the beach, and he looked out at the ship riding at anchor. Then he said a prayer. After that he put his ear down as if he were listening. At last he said, 'I know where the goods are. Go to the ship and you will find a hidden

bulkhead right in the bow. Look in that false compart-
ment, and you will find what you are searching for.' It
was just as he said. We found the goods and arrested the
captain of the ship."

I didn't credit Dr. Soumokil's tales of "white magic,"
but I did credit him as a man of character. Here we
were, East and West, thrown together in an isolation
block which forced us together in close companionship.
If the twain didn't quite have a meeting of minds, on
other occasions we acted as one.

Sitting on my cot with my Bible on my knees, I was
having my devotions one day. I was interrupted by a call
from behind the cells. "Pastor, pastor, come here quick!"

It was the voice of Dr. Soumokil. The Communist
prisoners were all locked up, but my cell was open. I
hurried to the rear to see what was wrong. There, on the
brick sidewalk Dr. Soumokil was kneeling and removing
a few of the bricks.

"Quick," he hollered, "Get a couple of sticks—see, over
there by the graves, and stand ready. I've got two rats
cornered in a hole here."

I armed myself and stood ready while he removed a
few more bricks and dirt.

"They are way down here. Give me one of those
sticks," he called. "I'll try and poke them out." But try as
he would, the rats had a nice corner where it was
difficult to reach them.

"Wait," I said, "I'll get my plastic bucket, and we'll
pour water down on them, and they will have to come up
or drown."

"OK," he exclaimed, "but hurry."

I came running with the bucket, dipped it in the water

reservoir in the bathroom, and poured the water down the hole. Out scrambled one rat!

Blam, wham! The rat race terminated for one 16-inch (tip of tail to nose) rodent.

"Now, let's get the other one," shouted Dr. Soumokil.

I ran to the reservoir and brought another pail of water. Another pailful and another. After the ninth pail of water, a sorry-looking, half-drowned rat appeared. Soumokil struck hard but missed.

With hearty shouts of "Kill him! Get him!" we pursued our enemy. The rocks richocheted off the cement walks and prison walls. We were so busily engaged in the war of rodents that we did not hear the cries at the doorway. "Hurry, unlock the door. Hurry, before you're too late! They're going to kill each other."

Just as the last deathblows were administered to the rat, an MP burst in through the door with two prisoners following him.

"Stop, what's going on," he shouted.

When he saw the two dead rats and Soumokil and I smiling, he breathed a deep sigh. "Ah," he said, "we were sure you two were killing one another."

We dug a little grave for the two dead animals, only about six feet from two graves of prisoners who had died or were executed during the Japanese occupation of Java. It was not a sacrilegious act. It was in back of the cells, and the dirt there was soft. We wished no more smell than necessary. In that hot climate it would have been only a matter of two days, and there would be a horrid smell. Not that there wasn't already. The heavily overloaded toilet was overflowing, and now all the prisoners of two blocks were using the fish pool. But there was no reason to make conditions worse.

If only some of my wartime buddies could see me now! At the end of the war when we talked a lot about what we were going to do when we got out of the service, I had announced that I was going to be a mortician. The gang in that two-story school building requisitioned by the U.S. 5th Army racked with laughter. "Digger Lovestrand! Say Digger, how's business? Dead! Dead? Yes, in this business we have stiff competition."

We were on the outskirts of Vienna, and those were cold, bitter February nights in 1946. The other company clerks had been digging into the records, counting their battle stars, purple hearts, and years of service, and coming up with a sum of points, so many and they could go home. Jim K. had a good plumbing job waiting for him. Chuck K. expected to take over his dad's delicatessen business. Gus J. planned to be an electrical engineer. Then they had asked me, "Hey, Lover, what are you going to do when you get out?"

I hadn't been ready to answer the first time the question came up, for I was undecided. But thinking over various jobs, I suddenly realized, *People are always dying. A mortician would always have steady work, depression or no depression.* The more I thought about it the more I liked it. At the next bull session I unveiled my idea.

After my discharge I did begin to make application to train as a mortician, but God had other plans for me—plans that led me to a prison in Djakarta.

The instrument He used was a missionary from Bolivia who was speaking at a church near my home. As the missionary spoke of the pagan Indians of South America and the need for missionaries to bring the message of salvation to them, a struggle commenced in my heart.

The realization came that God wanted me to put aside my plans to be an undertaker, to put aside the visions of a Cadillac, a beautiful home, a good bank account and all the other things I hoped to have some day.

I had argued with the Lord. Then I tried to bargain with Him. *Lord, if I'm an undertaker, I'll give you a tenth of my income. Lord, I'll give you 20 percent of my income if You'll let me be a mortician. Lord, someday when business is good, I'll even take on the support of a missionary all by myself.*

I resisted the appeal for volunteers at the end of the service and left the church feeling, *Now, that's that.*

Sleep was sound and sweet that night. In the morning my father, who had bought a farm, asked me to spread some manure out on the fields. This was in the days before my father purchased a mechanical manure spreader, so I had to spread it with a four-pronged pitchfork.

It was a beautiful day, and I began working with gusto. Then suddenly that awful, gnawing conviction had me in agony again. I thought to myself, *I'll just shake it like I did last night.*

I tried whistling. How I whistled! *I'll try singing*, I thought, and I sang lustily and sent the manure sailing through the air. Regardless of what I did that wretched, obnoxious feeling hung heavily on me. It became so intolerable that I finally prayed, *O Lord, I surrender. I can't bear it any longer.*

Peace, calm and tranquility filled my soul. It was decided. I was going to be a missionary.

The same peace was mine during the weeks and

months in prison. Not that it wasn't depressing to realize that the Communist defeat wasn't complete, that men like Dr. Subandrio were still in office and had the ear of President Sukarno.

The early euphoria which filled the prison when the Communist prisoners first arrived disappeared when the rest of us were still not released.

I heard by the prison rumors that Ambassador Green had been over to Merdeka Palace several times for consultations with Dr. Subandrio. But it was obvious that he had not been able to make much progress if my case was any indication.

At first I had been so hopeful. At one time the embassy provided me with a box of cheese crackers, another of graham crackers and a box of chocolates. I saved the chocolates for five days, hoping that I would be able to send them to Muriel via Mr. Sutjipto. But there were no interrogation sessions, so I gave up and shared them with my fellow prisoners.

In the depth of my despair I had to return again and again to my original call to the field, and I composed a verse in my prison ballad that spoke of just this:

> O Jesus, my Saviour, I've given you my all;
> You gave all without money or price;
> I've been apprehended while heeding your call,
> But true love demands sacrifice.
>
> In His love, Calvary love,
> Safe, secure, I rest where none can annoy;
> In His love, infinite love,
> I find comfort, peace, and joy!

19

Prisoner of Love

The clinking of keys, the sound of footsteps, or the squeak of a door would send prickling hot sensations over me. What was wrong with me?

My poor state of health began to worry me in October. The filariasis gave me a feeling of numbness in the back of the neck, parts of the back, my left leg and right arm. In the daytime, my eyelids felt unusually heavy.

A new sense of nervousness began to torture me. If it was the intention of my Indonesian hosts to break my resistance down by solitary confinement, perhaps they partially succeeded, but my loss of physical health accomplished more in this direction.

The interrogations, when they came, left me shaken. I dreaded them as a form of inquisition. More and more I prayed, *Lord, give me mental and physical strength, especially during the interrogations.*

These interrogations which took place on an average of every two weeks involved no physical cruelty. I was not beaten, and no bright lights were used. It was a kind of psychological third degree, however.

Usually five men were on the investigation committee. At times two or three would fire questions at me. One would laugh at my predicament. Another would call me a liar. One would pretend to be sympathetic, another angry and threatening, while another would lecture me. When this came from all sides at once, I became extremely nervous. The air would be rent with ranting and raving.

"We are doing the interrogating here, not you!"

"You just cooperate and answer like you're supposed to do."

I was always at fault. I was the one who had erred. I was not cooperating. I was always changing my story. I was a big liar. I was withholding information. I did not honor the law. I did not respect the officers of the law. I was the one who was prolonging the investigation.

One day my hecklers kept after me for about two hours and then had a lunch break. While we were sitting at the table eating, Mr. Moedjito pointed to a door in the room. Stuck into it was a long pin, like a hat pin, with a red flag on it. It was holding an old one rupiah bill.

"Isn't that a Communist symbol, heh, heh, heh?" Subcommissioner Hardjiman inquired, laughing nervously.

"Yes, of course," replied one of the others, and tried to change the subject.

These men were trying to be neutral, for the issue of final Communist domination or destruction had not been settled. The pin with the red flag was stuck through one of the old pieces of currency as a reminder of inflation, the inflation which the Communists blamed on the government.

After lunch the government attorney asked me to write down all the courses which were taught at the Bible school in Saowi. I listed quite a few, and then I said, "If I may ask, Sir, what connection do these courses have with my case?"

"It is none of your business what the connection is."

Mr. Sutjipto started a harangue, "Mr. Lovestrand, we are doing the questioning and not you. I'm tired of your arrogance and lack of cooperation. We are conducting this investigation for your own good. We are trying to help you, but you are not helping."

Mr. Martono chimed in, "So, he doesn't want to cooperate? Well, we can wait. Maybe he likes it in prison. Yes, we can wait a couple of weeks, a month, a year, two years."

It just seemed like I couldn't stand it any more. I was so agitated that I answered this last thrust of Mr. Martono.

"I am not afraid of the investigation. I haven't done anything wrong. I am not afraid of the law either. I have read the law of subversion of which I am accused, and it says the punishment is one year. But it is the interpretation of the law that you give that upsets me. You have been saying on the one hand that in a few days or a week this investigation would be finished, and now you say it could be two years."

Mr. Prasetyo, the attorney, drew himself up stiffly. "Shall we go on?" he said disdainfully.

"Yes," I answered.

Mr. Sutjipto had a countermove ready. "No," he said, "we can wait. Mr. Lovestrand does not want to cooperate, so we will wait until he is good and ready."

With that he collected the papers and started stuffing them into his briefcase. The MPs were called and told to take me back to prison. I rose wearily from my place. "I'm sorry, gentlemen," I apologized. "I became nervous and upset."

The MPs told me to come along.

"Good-by, gentlemen," I said with a try at a smile.

My smile was not returned.

The day following this investigation I had an especially bad day physically.

In letters to Muriel I tried to express myself, in guarded language, of course. It was during this period that I wrote to her:

My case seems to be going as fast as molasses in the winter, but I trust you won't be discouraged. Even if your board bill is high, mine is free! This reminds me that I think I am now probably thinner than any time since we have been married. It isn't necessarily a bad thing considering my weight was over 200 in Singapore in 1952 and is now the opposite extreme.

The Lord has given me some excellent lessons on faith out of *Living Letters*. "Because of our faith, He has brought us into this place of highest privilege where we now stand, and we confidently and joyfully look forward to actually becoming all that God has had in mind for us to be" (Rom. 5:2). This, of course, is our justification before God, but it has a special meaning to me now.

Why didn't I become an undertaker instead of this? Well, I can "blame" (really "praise") God as Paul did in I Corinthians 9:17, "God has picked me out and given me this sacred trust, and I have no choice."

I really do believe, Sweetheart, that the outcome of this experience will result in our good for "more than we would ever dare to ask or even dream of, infinitely beyond our highest prayers, desires, thoughts, or hopes."

So look up, Dear; God is planning great things for us, so that He will be the more glorified. Morticianing might have been more lucrative, but how dull compared to a missionary's life! And a mortician can't take it with him, where the results of our labors are eternal.

Sensing what I was going through, Muriel did all she could in her letters to cheer me up with accounts of the children and some of her own thoughts. She wrote:

> I know the days must be boring for you. I've been praying that the Lord would give you victory over discouragement and a definite sense of His presence ... I feel that all this is somehow working together with our request for a Spirit-filled ministry. I remember Arthur Mathews' statement (*Green Leaf in Drought Time*), "At first our thoughts were only on getting out, but now I am more concerned that we do not miss any of the gold the Lord has for us in this experience."
>
> I had a letter from Mr. Mortenson (mission director), the only mail I've received. He said that he had been in contact with both my folks and yours. . . . He said that never a day goes by but what there is intercession for us at the mission staff meeting.

Paradoxically, though my body suffered, my spirits began to soar. Paul's desire for the Thessalonians had been, "May the Lord bring you ever deeper into an understanding of the love of God and of the patience that comes from Christ" (II Thess. 3:5), and I prayed that this might be fulfilled in me. What did I know of the love of God? I knew that too often my love had been shallow and up and down, dependent on circumstances and feeling. God was teaching me a love which still loves when there is no love returned, a love which continues even when repaid by spite and hate.

I found that it was easier for me to love and forgive when feeling well, but it came hard when feeling bad physically. I wanted to learn the love of Christ who from the cross could even love those who crucified Him.

Shortly thereafter God gave me an opportunity to

speak to one of the guards about the Lord. Many of them had been friendly and attentive when I broached the subject of Jesus Christ. This man was even more open.

"God sent His only Son, Jesus Christ, into the world to be the Saviour of men. That means He can save you from sin, from the punishment of God," I said.

"How can He do that?" he asked.

"By taking our punishment on Himself," I explained, telling the man about the death of Christ on the cross, His burial and His resurrection from the dead. "He is alive, ready to forgive you and cleanse you from sin," I told him.

I showed him Scripture passages and then said, "Why don't you pray to God and ask for forgiveness? I'll help you."

Prisoner and guard bowed heads together. What did it matter that one bore a pistol at his side? He was a simple penitent at the bar of God. He was the one who needed to be set free. And praise God, he was, for he accepted Jesus Christ as his personal Saviour!

This made up for some of the anguish of heart I had had due to my physical weakness. And then it seemed like more "consolations" came my way. Although I continued to lack fruit and vegetables in my diet, I began to receive bread with my other food, morning and evenings. It is surprising how much those slices of bread meant to me.

Another boon was insect spray that came from the embassy. This was powerful enough to kill bedbugs, and these creatures had a way of crawling into my cell. Occasionally I would spot them on the walls. Frequently I caught them climbing on the outside of my mosquito net, and then there had been the ones which I didn't catch! They bit with a fury. And they would crawl back into the crevices of my cot, waiting for another feast. My score in killing these creatures was close to an "F" and I needed some help. The spray solved this problem.

Along with the spray came the brief information that American newspapers were carrying write-ups about my case. I expect the embassy wanted me to realize that I hadn't been forgotten.

I wrote wryly to my wife,

> The ambassador said that he had received many clippings from U.S. newspapers. . . . Well, I guess I'm getting popular; however, I would just as soon be without all this popularity. I do hope it stirs up . . . prayer among Christians. Perhaps it will draw them closer to the Lord.

The weaker I felt physically the more I wanted the support of my fellow Christians across the seas—in my home churches, in the mission and among unknown prayer warriors. Thank God, they were praying.

20

A Flag Held High

We had heard that Indonesian law states a foreigner can only be held eighty-one days without a formal charge. This is supposed to be three weeks without formal detention and then not more than sixty days of formal detention. This is what is called investigative justice. In my case the wheels of justice ground to a halt, for the eighty-one days passed without either a charge or a release.

My interrogations continued, though not always at the same place. On October 29 I was brought to a house in the suburb at Kebajoran Baru. A tape recorder was on the table, and while one may have been used before, placed somewhere out of sight, here it was in front of me.

Maybe my interrogators were afraid of the tape recorder or whoever might listen to its recording later. As we started I felt that they were deliberately trying to make it hard for me, and the tension in the room kept increasing as they beset me with a storm of questions. While this was confusing, I could still pick out the easier ones to answer and let the others slide by. I couldn't possibly answer them all because they were coming too fast.

Suddenly they came to the question toward which

they had been building, "What do you know about the Kebar uprising?"

At this point they all began to concentrate on this one question, needling and laughing at me.

"Kebar uprising?" I inquired. "I did not know there was an uprising in the Kebar." This is the grassy upland region in the "Bird's Head" due west of Manokwari.

"What? You did not know there was an uprising in the Kebar?"

"You only lived sixty miles away? Why wouldn't you know about it?"

"You, an intelligent man, a university graduate, and you don't know?"

"Of course, you know," said Mr. Moedjito. "You are a big liar."

"Tell us!" demanded the attorney, Mr. Prasetyo.

"I'm sorry, I don't know," I answered.

"Of course, you know. Now tell us. You've been living thirteen years among these people. Surely they've told you something."

"Come on, you're a missionary, and you're not supposed to lie. Tell us what you know about the uprising in the Kebar."

They fired more questions, insinuations and abusive comments at me. Then the attorney demanded again, "Answer me!"

This latest volley tore my nerves to the breaking point. I shouted, "I don't know," and unconsciously I slammed my fist down on the table in front of me.

The table wobbled, and then, *Smash!* The fist of the attorney landed on the table, and he screeched, "Who do you think you are? If anyone is going to pound the table around here, it will be us and not you!"

The wobbly table which had been shaken by my blow was crippled by his more powerful one. It staggered, and the brass leg to his left slipped out of place and fell to the floor. I was startled, and I think that the committee was too. Someone grabbed the table to steady the tape recorder, and someone else stooped to make repairs.

Flushed with their exertions, they turned on me. "What do you mean by such actions?" they asked.

"I'm sorry," I said. "I didn't even realize that I pounded the table. I guess I was only trying to emphasize the fact that I didn't know."

Things simmered down a little, and then Mr. Moedjito started up. "*Tuan,*" he asked, "do you know how to fix radios?"

"No, Sir," I answered.

"Then do you know how to destroy radios?" he badgered.

"Yes, Sir," I answered, and his face lighted up momentarily. I smiled and continued, "All you have to do is take an axe to the radio."

No one else smiled, that is on the outside, but I believe the others enjoyed Mr. Moedjito's discomfiture.

About a week later I was hauled to the Office of West Irian Affairs where Komisaris Hardjanto told me, "We would like to settle your case as quickly as possible. I think that we could finish it up in about a week if only you would cooperate with the investigating committee. There is no need for you to become angry when they ask you questions. Just stick to the facts, and don't always change your story."

I could not think of a time when I did not cooperate with them ever since they yielded to my request to see either a lawyer or the ambassador. I had not refused to answer any questions. I really was not angry with any of the interrogators, though when they frayed my nerves, I did speak out forthrightly. Perhaps they thought this was too bold and nervy. How could he charge me with changing my story? It was a simple one which I had told over and over like a broken record.

After my brief visit with Komisaris Hardjanto I was escorted over to a building on Cassuari Street. There I found the investigating committee gathered and with them Robert Rich, vice-consul from the embassy, and a Colonel Ethel of the U.S. Army. I had noticed the Americans leaving Mr. Hardjanto's office before he called me in.

Colonel Ethel began talking to me. Before long, I sat gulping with amazement. He was parroting almost word for word the same speech I had heard from Komisaris Hardjanto only fifteen or twenty minutes before.

What was he? Some legal aid of the embassy? Why was he there? Was he seeking to impress the committee by his admonitions to me? As I sat there stunned, I said to myself, *Colonel Ethel, whose side are you on? Are you so naïve that you believe the lies of these men? What are you trying to do—conduct their brainwashing for them?*

I was hurt and irked and wondered why he took the trouble to come. He could have given the committee a lecture on how to treat a suspect, but instead he was lecturing me.

When I wrote my wife about it later, I said,

> The last time I saw Bob Rich, almost two weeks ago, he had a Colonel Ethel with him. If you happen to see Bob, tell him I would appreciate it a whole lot more if he would bring along a Muriel instead of an Ethel!

I had asked her to get new pictures and to apply for new passports for us since the government had taken our former ones. I also wanted her to check up on the health certificates and shots for herself and the children. This was on my mind because our old passports were due to expire on November 30.

I felt that if the investigation could only be completed, we might be asked to leave the country in a hurry.

Bob Rich was able to advance me some local currency for some of my needs in prison. I knew that I could buy a few commodities at the prison store by placing an order through a guard, but up to this time I lacked funds.

At my one interrogation in November, Mr. Martono asked me sarcastically if the Bible has anything to say about lying. This was because I had my Bible with me. I carried it with me whenever I went out of prison, and it became a sort of symbol to me of all the promises I had claimed from it. I looked forward to those promises being fulfilled at any time, and holding that Bible was like holding my flag high.

Many times when I had to wait on the arrival of the committee, I would read Scripture portions which would lift my spirits. The Bible gave me confidence that I would be vindicated and that deliverance and victory were ultimately mine.

Conversation turned somehow to the army, and then Mr. Martono asked, "Where does the U. S. Army train its officers?"

"At West Point, New York," I replied.

"And the navy?"

"At Annapolis, Maryland."

"The air force?"

"At Denver, Colorado," I answered.

"And the FBI?" Martono inquired.

"I don't know," I returned.

Then Mr. Martono looked at some of the other committee members, winked and smiled knowingly.

That day, November 6, I signed two sets of investigation papers, and that completed my interrogation until December. This made November a good month, for I was under much less tension. On November 22 one of the guards tipped me off, "There is a doctor at the front office to see you." Half an hour later I was told to come out. When I walked into the office of Captain Slamet Sentosa, the jail warden, I met an Indonesian doctor of Chinese extraction and also Dr. Schaefer of the U. S. Embassy. Mr. Rich was there and the very familiar faces of Mr. Moedjito, Mr. Sutjipto and Mr. Prasetyo.

The doctors examined me and found me in reasonable condition. I had noticed considerable improvement myself, far different from the way I felt three weeks before. I still had some spells of nervousness, but they did not come as often and were shorter in duration.

The embassy doctor said he would send me vitamins. Mr. Rich mentioned that he had brought a letter from Muriel, but he had to have it censored first.

After this break in prison routine, I was left to my own devices, passing the days of detention as best I could. I wondered when the investigation would be complete for my mentors had promised that when it was finished I could begin to have visits from Muriel. I had hopefully handed in a letter to her which they held and did not deliver until much later. It said:

> Other prisoners with very serious accusations and
> convictions against them have had visits from their

wives in less than a week after they entered here. I
think I know the best way for you to get permission to
visit me and that is to go to the Djaksa Agung
("Public Prosecutor") office and pester them until you
get it. But you decide for yourself if you would like to
give it a try or not ... last year a Christian prisoner here
got visits from his wife on the 24th, 25th, and 26th of
December because these are all holidays on the Christian calender. I mention this so that you can make your
request, personally, to the office of the Djaksa Agung—
if I'm still locked up.

Maybe the committee is finished. I hope so! Well,
sabar sadja, ("just be patient") and we'll see how the
mop flops!

Each morning before breakfast I read four pages in my
Thompson Chain Reference Bible, and after breakfast I
read an epistle or two in *Living Letters*. In II Thessalonians 3:1-3, 5 I found help and instruction:

> "Pray first that the Lord's message will spread rapidly
> and triumph wherever it goes [that is, what comes first,
> not our own personal needs] ... Pray too that we will be
> saved out of the clutches of evil men [how real this was
> to me], ... May the Lord bring you ever deeper into ...
> the patience that comes from Christ."

He had learned patience, and I should be ready to do
so too.

21

The Valley of the Shadow

An interrogation was ending, and my head pounded furiously. Such a headache, and yet I couldn't understand it. It was December. True I was having my fourth interrogation within six days, but these sessions shouldn't have given me a headache. They had moved along rapidly and in a friendly way. Mr. Martono said we were nearly finished.

I was glad when the questioning was completed, and I could go back to my cell. By early evening I was aware of a fever. I went to bed early but not to rest. During the night the fever climbed while I tossed and turned. The next morning I was understandably tired. My fever continued for days, rising each evening and dropping down by morning.

At least five or six times I asked help of the guards and three times sent notes to the prison office asking for medical attention. The office responded by sending me a few APC pills, and once a male nurse came along and gave me a shot of penicillin. Even though I suspected that I had malaria, I was desperate enough to try anything. I had written asking for malarial drugs without success. Fellow prisoners chided me for not giving a bribe to secure help, but I didn't want to descend to that.

The tenth night of my illness, December 16 I think it was, my temperature went extremely high. The next morning I managed somehow to drag my mattress out into the sun to dry. It, as well as my sheets and clothing, had been soaked with perspiration. I recall that Dr. Soumokil helped me by washing the bottom sheet and some of my clothes.

He was most solicitous about the condition of my health and kept checking on me daily.

"Someday I'd like to work with you," he said.

"How do you mean?" I asked.

"In Christian work," he replied. "If I get out of here, I would like to go to seminary and prepare for Christian work. My father always wanted me to be a minister, but I rejected the idea. Years later when I was captured and had my trial, I was condemned to death. At that time I promised God that if He would save me from death, I would be willing to go into the ministry. My death sentence has not been carried out yet! I'm still hoping for a chance to fulfill my promise."

Prisoners have a lot of waiting to do, but they never get accustomed to it. My long wait for medical help began to draw to a close on the twelfth day of my illness. The American Embassy secured visiting privileges and sent Mr. Diefenbach and a Dr. Schaefer to check on my health. Mr. Martono accompanied them as well as an Indonesian doctor.

They met me in the prison office, and Dr. Schaefer asked, "Do you have a fever now?"

I answered, "The night before last I was really burning

up, but the fever went down. Today it feels about normal, but I am very weak."

He took my temperature, and looking at the thermometer, passed it on to the other doctor. "It is 102°F." he said. Then he remarked, "If it is 102°F. now, I wonder how high it was the other night."

"I don't know, Sir," I replied. "I have had as high as 105.5° with malaria back in West Irian."

"I'm sorry that I don't have any equipment with me to take samples or specimens now," the doctor said. "If I am allowed to get them, I'll be back on Monday. Neither do I have any malaria drugs with me, but here's a little aspirin."

The next day was Sunday, and for the first time I was given permission to attend the Protestant service conducted by Ex-colonel Simbolon. I had often listened to these from a distance because they were held in a room just over the wall from the isolation block. I tried to get up this morning, but I was simply too sick. I stayed on my cot.

By evening I was feeling somewhat better. Dr. Soumokil had come back from the service to tell me that I was invited to preach the prisoners' Christmas sermon.

Though I was still feverish I wrapped a sheet around me and made my round of prayers with the men in our block. I had been doing this regularly each evening about six o'clock, going from cell to cell and praying with each one. I did this every evening except one, and that time I was just too weak to walk.

Monday morning the guards told me to go up to the front office, and I barely made it. I sat down for a while to regain my strength. The doctors had not come to me; I would have to make a trip to the Public Prosecution Department to see them. There I met Dr. Schaefer again, and his laboratory technician, Bob Critch. The doctor examined me and found my temperature stood at 104°F. He started to write out a medical report while Bob took blood samples.

After the doctor and technician had left, the Public Prosecution Department officials scanned the report left in their hands. Mr. Soederadjat and Mr. Sutjipto of the Immigration Department tried to figure out the English terminology Dr. Schaefer had used, but they gave up. They turned to me and said, "Here, you translate this for us."

I was glad to do so. The report said that I was suffering from either typhus or malaria, and that I should be transferred to a hospital as soon as possible. It ended with the words, "If this man does not receive prompt medical attention, his life will be jeopardized."

They broke out in laughter when I read the last sentence. I failed to see the humor in this, but then perhaps I was biased!

One of them stretched himself and said, "Mr. Lovestrand, are you ready to go on with the investigation today?"

"Well, Sir, the doctor said I have quite a high fever. I think if he says that I am ill, I'd better not be investigated today."

"In that case we will not get finished in time for you to leave the country by Christmas." He sounded so disappointed!

It was a tight turn of the screw, but I knew that I could not take questioning that morning. "Perhaps my health is more important than leaving the country," I said.

I was escorted back to prison. During the rest of the day I kept hoping that someone would come and take me to a hospital, but nothing happened.

At six o'clock I prayed with the prisoners and went to bed. By eight o'clock I was feeling flushed, and I knew that another ordeal was starting. In anticipation of a high fever I had placed a bottle of drinking water and a bucket of wash water near my cot. Now I took aspirin, but it gave me no relief.

Chills started, and I shivered and shook. Then I became hot and burning. I shed my sheet, then my pajamas. I took my washcloth and bathed my body. That gave some relief. My head ached and felt so hot. I laid the damp cloth on my forehead. When the water had evaporated, I repeated the operation, over and over.

Throughout the evening I burned with a fever more ferocious than I had ever experienced. My throat started feeling dry, and I took a sip of boiled water. By one o'clock in the morning I had finished drinking the two quarts of drinking water that I had by my bedside.

At a little past one o'clock I began to perspire and get cold. The chills came. I put on my pajamas and my sheet. I still shivered. I reached out of the mosquito net and grabbed all my clothing and my towel. These, too, I put over me.

Gradually I began to feel warmer. Then perspiration began dripping from my pores. My pillow became soaked. My pajamas stuck to my body. The chills came and went. I found that I was having difficulty breathing. Each inhalation seemed a herculean task. I remember praying, *O Lord, how easy it would be to stop breathing, and then You could take me home. How wonderful it would be to come into Your presence.*

That long grim night probably witnessed one of my longest private conversations with the Lord. My desires seemed to hover between earth and heaven, between being with my family and my Saviour. Death didn't seem menacing at all. On the contrary, I felt like I was on the threshold of a beautiful, intimate contact with the glory and love of Jesus Christ. I had no fear. "Lord," I prayed, "I long to be with You."

As I prayed there on my wet, uncomfortable mattress, Muriel and the children also came to my mind. I had the assurance that if the Lord took me, He would care for them. At the same time I had the sense that perhaps the Lord had something more for me to do. I struggled to breathe. Then it came a little easier.

The last time I looked at my watch it was five o'clock. The guards opened the cell doors, and I knew that meant five-thirty. I could hear the other prisoners going out and taking their baths. Never mind, I stayed in bed. Just before seven I got up. Breakfast would be coming, not that I had any appetite for it.

Taking off my wet pajamas, I put on underwear and a pair of shorts. What exertion! And even the clothes I changed into were damp.

As I took off the wet sheets and hung them to dry, I staggered and nearly fell. I struggled with the mattress and managed to turn it over. The bottom side had a seven inch circle of wetness which had soaked through from the night before. I flopped down anyway, exhausted.

Rattle, clang. The circular food containers were being dropped down beside our doors, a series of little pans one on top of the other, a different kind of food in each section. When I had rested some, I decided I should try and get some food down. Ugh! It was insipid, but I forced some of it down.

There was something I had to do, and I decided I should do it while I still had some strength. I pulled the wobbly bench over, got out a pad of paper and began writing. The letter I scribbled has since been lost, but it went something like this:

DEAR MURIEL,

If I have to go through another night like last night, I don't think I'll be able to pull through. It was the worst night I have ever spent in my life. If the Lord should take me home, I hope that you will take the children back to the States and not try to go on alone here. I think your first responsibility is to the children.

If God should lead you to another man, I trust that you will make him as happy as you have me . . .

I finished the letter and put it among my toilet articles. I lay down on the cot again and closed my eyes.

I awoke to a knock at my door. A guard was calling me, and I was wanted up front. "I am too weak to go," I said. "Would you kindly call another MP, so that I can lean on both your shoulders?"

He disappeared but came back in about five minutes with a companion and a stretcher. They carried me out to the office and then to a waiting automobile. I sat in a front seat and was driven to the Public Prosecution Department. Somehow I managed to get out, climb that familiar staircase and walk down the long hall. When I walked into the office of the bureau of subversion, Muriel was there!

She rushed toward me and helped me to a chair. I gave her a weak squeeze. That was all I could manage—no smile, no words. I was at the end of my tether.

22

Place of Refuge

*Mr. Diefenbach and Dr. Tom Woods, a military at-*taché, awaited me in Mr. Soederadjat's office. Mr. Sutjipto and Mr. Soederadjat watched the medical examination closely.

Had the doctor realized how weak I was, I don't believe he would have asked me to move to another chair. I did attempt the move, and I made it.

Though exhausted, I managed to tell them what a terrible night I had had. Then Dr. Woods said, "Your blood test revealed that you have malaria, and it was the highest concentration of malarial parasites that we have ever seen under a microscope. Now we are trying to get you into a hospital."

A report from the embassy that I read later said that it was discovered that I was suffering from two different strains of malaria, and the disease had progressed to the stage where the hemoglobin concentration went down to 6 grams per 100 cc's.

I noticed a glass of tea standing on one of the desks, so I said to Mr. Soederadjat, "I'm so thirsty. May I have a drink?"

I was dreadfully dry. I felt as if I had cotton in my

mouth. No wonder, for during the night I had lost so much liquid through perspiration.

"Yes," answered Mr. Soedradjat, handing me the tea.

I drank it down. When it was gone, he asked, "Would you like another glass of tea?"

"Yes, please," I replied.

Soon another was brought to me. Then Mr. Diefenbach said, "I'll go to the embassy nearby and get you some fruit juice if you'd like." I couldn't refuse this kind offer, so away he went. Dr. Woods also went out to see if he could arrange a place for me in a hospital.

I sat and talked with Muriel. She said, "I didn't know until two days ago that you had been sick. It was just yesterday that Mr. Rich came to the house and told me how ill you have been. He told me that the embassy officials had not been allowed to see you for three weeks. When they were finally granted permission the Indonesian authorities said, 'Perhaps you had better bring a doctor with you.'

" 'Why? Is Mr. Lovestrand sick?'

" 'Well, yes, he is.' They had been worried about you but had no way of getting to you."

Mr. Diefenbach reappeared with a thermos of ice water, some canned fruit, several kinds of juices and a quart of milk. The milk was especially delicious. Ummm! It was good. And my thirst was finally quenched.

Muriel and I talked about the prison and the children for an hour before Dr. Woods arrived back.

"Success!" he said. I've arranged a room for you in a military hospital."

Mr. Soederadjat phoned the hospital to check on it, and then he said, "It's OK, he may go."

Soon we were on our way. I went in a jeep with Mr.

Sutjipto and a guard. Muriel, Mr. Diefenbach and Dr. Woods rode in another car.

On arrival at the hospital I was taken to an examination room where I was checked in. I was feeling weak, but the tea and milk I had had at the Public Prosecutor's Department certainly helped.

The day before I had had a temperature of 104°F, but at this point my temperature was 99°F.

Mr. Sutjipto asked the examining doctor, "What is his temperature?"

"Normal," answered the doctor.

As if thunderstruck Mr. Sutjipto repeated, "Normal?" Then he jotted this information down in his notebook.

And I thought, *Ah, Mr. Sutjipto, why do you have to be so suspicious? I weighed in at the prison office, and I'm down to around 145 pounds from my normal 180. Isn't that enough to show you that I'm ill?*

I said nothing. It would have been futile.

Before long I was taken into a section of the hospital called the Pavilion. This spacious hospital was built many years ago by the Dutch. I was placed in a room with a view out on a wide veranda. The veranda went all around the building, its pillars of white supporting the roof. It was open, free and roomy. My spirits lifted.

Dr. Woods, Dale Diefenbach, and Muriel stayed about half an hour and then left. I began to relax in my pleasant surroundings, so different from my cell.

Supper came about six o'clock, and the nurse brought me two quinine tablets. I thanked the Lord for His goodness and for the food. Then I ate.

An hour or so later another patient strolled into my room. He introduced himself as Lt. Col. Sudjatno. Then he asked pleasantly who I was and why I was in the hospital.

"I have malaria and my hemoglobin is down to six," I replied. "Oh, and my name is Lovestrand. Maybe you remember reading sometime ago in the newspapers about a missionary suspected of being an agent of the CIA. That was I."

Suddenly the officer was gone. I wanted to shout after him, "But it's not true." He hadn't given me a chance to finish what I had to say. He would be spreading word around the hospital that an alien agent was in room No. 5, and this made me feel very depressed.

I had difficulty getting to sleep that night. I kept thinking about Lt. Col. Sudjatno. Normally I wouldn't tell a stranger what I had told him. I was afraid that I hadn't been clear in what I said. Perhaps I had given the wrong impression. Maybe he was an agent of the intelligence. I was disturbed about my being so irrational, and it wasn't until after twelve midnight that I slept.

The next morning I noticed my guard posted on the veranda to watch me, and my feelings slumped further. Wasn't it enough that there were guards at the gates? Did they have to follow me right into the hospital, too?

Muriel came in and brightened me up.

"Hello, Dearie," she said. "You're looking much better now! I've brought you some clean clothing and some food."

"Tell me, Honey," I said, "whatever happened to you and the children? Your letters didn't explain enough."

At last I heard her story. After our separation up in the mountains the days dragged slowly by. She had brought no school books along for the children because we had been told in Manokwari that we would be out of the country in a few days.

"Let's look in all the suitcases," she told the children. "Let's see what we can find. We are going to have school."

Their excited search yielded only one pencil, a crayon and a little paper. With these, plus a Bible and a children's storybook, they started their lessons. No wonder most of the work was arithmetic.

After Welas and Suwardi left, the local police station assigned the guards. New shifts came every eight hours, and to the children the "changing of the guard" was always an important event.

Welas and Suwardi had always been kind to them, understanding how children like to play. Some of the new men insisted that they stay right near the house and this deprived them of walks in the nearby rice fields.

Muriel witnessed to the guards, and though most of them were Muslims, they often were ready to listen to her tell about Jesus Christ. For many it was their first contact with Christianity.

One day the family was abruptly transferred to Djakarta and placed in detention in the same house I had occupied a few days before. Muriel found that the days dragged, but our children enjoyed the company of two small Indonesian children living in the same compound. After daily lessons were completed, they played games and sang Indonesian songs. But in their quieter moments would come the off-repeated question, "Where is Daddy?"

Their mommy would reply, "I don't know, Dear. We must just trust God to take care of him."

Daily in their prayers they would commit the care of

their loved one to the One whom they could trust implicitly.

Six days after my fortieth birthday and imprisonment, Muriel had her birthday. The children drew a birthday card for her and presented it to her behind the closed bedroom door, singing, "Happy birthday to you!"

That evening she had her birthday present—a visit from Mr. Sutjipto, Mr. Martono and Mr. Moedjito. They sat down and began to ask questions.

"The children must miss their father terribly, don't they?"

"They do, but of course, he has often been gone before," she parried. "We have been in Christian work which has often involved separation. Of course, we don't like it, but we have had to get used to it."

"Don't you wish you knew where your husband is?"

Of course, she did, but she wondered what they were seeking to do. She told me that if she had known I was actually in solitary confinement that she would not have been able to answer so freely. She avoided a direct answer.

"It doesn't really matter. I know that God is with him wherever he is and that He will take care of him."

Mr. Martono now began to ask questions, while Mr. Sutjipto jotted down notes. The gist of his questioning was aimed at implicating Muriel for her failure to report the rumors of trouble which had been rampant in Manokwari before the rebellion.

Why didn't she report the rumors? Why wasn't she afraid when the shooting started? Why didn't she ask for police protection? Did she know anyone who was dissatisfied with the government? The interrogation went on for two hours.

After the men left, it took her a long time to quiet her thoughts and get to sleep. On her part she had asked them for school books for the children. Would they send her supplies so she could teach them? Would she face more interrogations?

Instead of the books, she received a message the following afternoon that she should pack and be ready to leave. As she readied the suitcases, she wondered, "Where are we going now?"

The next day American embassy officials arrived with the men from the Department of West Irian Affairs. It was not until then that Muriel learned that the purpose of this visit was to release her and to turn the family over to the care of the embassy. Official papers were signed, and within a few minutes the captives walked out to an embassy car and freedom. They had been in custody for almost two months. They learned that their destination was a missionary guest house where friends were waiting to greet them and hear the tale of what had happened since their disappearance.

23

On Again–Off Again

How good it was to get caught up on all the news! I already had heard that the family had been able to move into a partially furnished embassy home near the international school. Embassy personnel had been kindness personified in seeking to help Muriel settle in. Missionaries of The Christian and Missionary Alliance loaned her linens and dishes.

"The house is lovely," Muriel told me. "It's the nicest place I've ever lived in on the field. All I need there is a husband!"

"How have the children been taking it?" I asked.

"When I first found out that you had actually been placed in prison, I hesitated to say anything to them about it. I thought it would be easier for them in school, but I couldn't really keep it from them too long.

"One day I had heard a little boy ask Danny, 'Don't you have a daddy?' He answered, 'Of course, I have a daddy!'

"The boy persisted, 'Where is he?'

"Danny refused to answer that one. He was stumped, but he wasn't going to admit that you were in prison. There was a silence for a few moments.

"Then Joan, who had been listening, piped up nonchalantly, 'Oh, our daddy's in town.' "

She turned the conversation, "Let me tell you about Dr. Mortenson's visit. At the end of November I had a letter from him saying that he felt that as general director of the mission he should come here and that he was asking Cal Roesler, our field chairman, to meet him in Djakarta.

"The same day I received his letter I was in the embassy renewing my passport. Ambassador Green, hearing that I was in the building, invited me into his office. He told me how sorry he was that you were still being detained and mentioned that he had just received word of Mr. Mortenson's intended visit.

"The ambassador told me that he would plan a luncheon for him on December 9 and that I was invited to attend. I saw him again at the American Thanksgiving service. He stopped to shake hands with me, saying, 'I'm sorry that we couldn't have given you a happier Thanksgiving. I hope we can give you a better Christmas.'

"A few days later Mr. Rich came to the home, definitely excited. He said, 'I'm sure that you will have a better Christmas. I have definite promises now that your husband will be released within eight or ten days!'

"He asked me not to say anything about it, for the Indonesian officials were anxious to let you go very quietly. If news were to get out, it might spoil everything."

"Spoil everything?" I exclaimed. "They put the news out as they call it, and before it is published, they are ready with a revised second edition! It was back in September that I asked Mr. Martono if he thought my investigation was finished, and he said, 'Yes, it is. Now it is in the hands of those higher up.' Then in November Komisaris Legowo said that the investigation was completed and that he saw no reason why I could not be released in a week or ten days. Here it is nearly Christmas, and the guessing game goes on."

"We certainly were guessing about the time Mr. Mortenson arrived," Muriel said. "The ten days Mr. Rich had told me about were nearly up, and I was hoping that the end was in sight. Cal Roesler and Vernon Neigenfind of the Inter-Missions business office drove me to the airfield to meet him. I took the children. On the way they attempted to drive by the prison, but they found the street barricaded with barbed wire.

"At the airport the plane came in, and it was easy to find Mr. Mortenson. He's so tall! He came toward us, saying, 'Hello, Muriel! What's the latest word on Harold?' And then, looking at Joel, he said, 'Now let's see—you're Joel—and here are Joan and Steve and Danny.'

"At the Protestant Guest House we sat and talked, and one of the first things he said was that we are being remembered daily in prayer at mission headquarters. Then he mentioned talking to your mother and my mother on the phone. 'Muriel,' he said, 'your mother is so sweet and confident about everything that I can understand where you get your steadiness.'

"Mr. Mortenson wanted to see you, if possible, but he waited to get advice from the embassy on this. When they urged him not to make any approaches, he limited himself to encouraging me and talking to Cal about field matters."

"What is happening in West Irian?" I asked.

"They are still not around the corner in Manokwari," she replied. "The pastor of the church in Manokwari ran away, along with a good many other people, and it has been hard to carry on the work there. But a new missionary couple, Doug and Julie Miller, are just coming out to the field. They will have a few days here in Djakarta in early January."

Mr. Mortenson was most considerate in planning to visit our children, Tim and Andrea, in Manila with the latest news from Djakarta. They had been wondering whether or not we would be released in time for Christmas and if in that case we would all be together for the vacation period. Mr. Mortenson could not give them a definite answer to this question, but he told them that they should be proud of their mother. He admired her composure and felt that it was a powerful testimony to the Lord's presence with her.

Christmas was coming, but little preparation had been made in the house at No. 13, Mulawarman. Muriel wondered if she should buy gifts and decorations. Finally, she decided to buy some lightweight gifts which could be easily packed and taken along should I be released.

Mr. Rich had come to see the family again, this time to inform Muriel that I was being released and that we could all leave quietly on Christmas Eve for Bangkok. This was Dr. Woods' choice because he knew of a good hospital there, and he felt that the short trip would not be too strenuous for a person in my condition.

Muriel packed for the family, took the children for cholera shots, attended the Christmas program at school, took the children to a Christmas party at the ambassador's residence and helped Joan get to the television studio where her class was putting on a special program. Mr. Neigenfind arranged the air tickets. There was rejoicing in the air, but it was rejoicing tinged with a little doubt. Had there not been many promises before? And this promise, though so definite, was only verbal. It still was not down in black and white.

As she continued packing and cleaning house, American officials were contacting their counterparts in the Indonesian government for final confirmation of the release. The answer they received was a blow, "Our superiors have changed their minds. We have been told to wait and not let Mr. Lovestrand go yet."

An abject embassy official broke the news to Muriel. She accepted it calmly, but to her mind came the story of the Matthews' family in China. So often they had been tantalized by the Communists who held out "specious promises of release."

Tim and Andrea had given up on the rest of the family arriving in the Philippines, and they had accepted an invitation to the home of school friends.

Muriel discovered how largehearted her Djakarta friends really were. When they heard that her hopes had been dashed, they rallied around to make this Christmas one to remember. They shared Christmas decorations. Some sent flowers. Gifts came in for the children. The family was invited to the home of Dr. Keith Parks for Christmas dinner.

I was not forgotten. On Christmas Day Muriel came to the hospital, and around her clustered four little figures. The guards had allowed the children in to see me!

They trooped into the room, carrying a Christmas basket full of fruit, nuts, cake and other goodies. Little Joel clung to his mother and was very shy of me. It was the first time in three and a half months that I had seen them, and Joel seemed the most changed of them all. Instead of a baby, here was a little boy. Very little, of course, and very unsure of this daddy in such a strange place.

The children were only allowed to stay for a few minutes. When they had stepped out, Muriel said to me, "The embassy officials were very upset when the promises of your release didn't materialize. They have been treated very poorly all this time. It must be humiliating for them to be snubbed in this way. They are not giving up, however. You may be sure that they intend for you to stay in the hospital. One of them said to me, 'Your husband will only be sent back to prison over the ambassador's dead body.' He's really concerned about you and has done everything humanly possible for you."

24

Missing Pieces

Joel had come along with Muriel to visit me in the
hospital. He was as shy as ever, lurking over in a corner
and unwilling to approach me. He started to climb up on
a screen, slipped and fell to the floor. He started to howl.
In an instant I was there and picked him up in my arms
and comforted him. In turn he hugged me tight, and I
knew that I had bridged the gap.

Muriel found the restrictions lessening around me.
Although the Public Prosecutor's Department had only
granted permission to her to visit me once a week, the
hospital urged her to bring me food every day. When she
brought my meals, the guards told her to bring them in.
I noticed that other prisoners in the hospital, for there
were some under guard like myself, were visited by their
whole families, and sure enough, when Muriel brought
the other children with her on the weekends, they were
allowed in.

We observed the length of time allowed other visitors
and found it to be an hour. Muriel lengthened her visits
to an hour as well.

To my surprise my guard disappeared, and when there
was no replacement, I mentioned it to another patient.

"This is an army hospital," he explained. "There are

military guards at the gates, and you will see some uniformed guards about the wards. But your guard came in civilian clothes. The fact that he was a plainclothesman, wearing a pistol irked the CQ. Ever since October it has been against the law for anyone in ordinary civilian dress to carry arms. The penalty for disobeying this order is severe.

"The MP came up to your guard and asked, 'What are you doing here?'

"He replied, 'I'm watching Mr. Lovestrand.' At that, the MP told him to leave and put on a uniform if he wanted to guard you. He left, and I haven't seen him come back."

I never saw him again either, and it was a great relief to me.

The Public Prosecutor's Department may have decided not to get into an interdepartmental dispute. They still were responsible for my safe custody, but all my papers had been completed and forwarded to the Ministry of Foreign Affairs.

Whenever Muriel would ask when I might be released, the answer was, "Soon—a short time." The question in our minds was how long "short" would prove to be. Somebody of high rank was holding my case up.

With the beginning of the new year of 1966, we again had a surge of hope that we were approaching the end of my captivity. Doug Miller and his wife arrived fresh from the States and told us about the round-the-clock schedule of prayer for me in TEAM headquarters. It was a humbling experience to know that so many were making sacrifices in prayer for us, and we were grateful.

I prayed that if release were near, I would not forget in the light what God had taught me in the dark.

Somewhere I had read the reverse of this, to the effect of "Don't forget in the dark what God has taught you in the light." For me it seemed to work the other way, for I have learned my most important lessons in the hardest places.

Although we thought at the beginning of January that the end was in sight, we were badly mistaken; after a few weeks passed, I seemed to be no closer to release than ever. My health had improved, but I still was held at the hospital. Muriel determined to try going directly to President Sukarno to ask for my release. As she weighed the matter, she realized that there were chances involved that he might be kind and considerate but also that he might brush the request aside. However, when she tried, she found that she could not secure an audience with the president. With students demonstrating in the streets, prices skyrocketing and the people demanding a change in government, he had more important things on his mind than the release of one illegally-held American.

It seemed that no other official wanted to take the responsibility for signing my release and laying himself open to the charge of being pro-American. The anti-Communist party was still strictly nationalistic and unaligned. I was not their concern.

At this point a fellow American tried to come to the rescue. Pat Price, an American university student, had become acquainted with the president in Cairo and she decided to use her powers of persuasion. The first time she brought the subject up in his presence, he claimed that he knew very little about the case. She immediately volunteered to bring him the pertinent papers on the case so that he could review them that weekend. Of course, when she went to get the papers from the Foreign Office, they would not send them to the president.

In disgust she returned to President Sukarno.

"I couldn't get the papers," she said. "Your man wouldn't release them."

"It doesn't matter. I already know all about the case," the president said, scowling. He was obviously in no mood to discuss the release of prisoners.

"But when are you going to release him? Don't you know he has been held for six months without any charges?"

"I know it," the president snapped.

"Don't you know that he has a wife and six children?" she ventured.

"I know that, too," retorted *Bung* ("Brother") Karno.

She tried once again, "But when are you going to release him?"

At this, the president lost patience. "Look here," he yelled, grabbing a couple of papers on his desk, "I've already signed two death sentences this morning. Do you want me to sign a third?"

When the result of this interview reached Muriel, my wife lost interest in any further attempts in this direction. Moreover, she did not tell me about it, fearing that it might upset me.

Her daily visits to me—usually with a basket of clothes and food—were by bus. By the time she had been packed on and pushed down the aisle, she could barely get off at the right stop.

"This is one way of really getting next to the people literally," she told me with a laugh.

The bus took one hour from the house into Djakarta,

and she took a *betjak* ("pedicab") from the bus stop to the hospital. This three-wheeled carriage has the seats in front and a man pedaling behind. By the time she piled in with four children, it must have been quite a sight to see. Once, leaving the hospital on a rainy Sunday afternoon, the *betjak* driver accidentally hit one of the numerous deep ruts in the street, and his passengers tumbled out, surprised, a bit muddy, but unhurt.

Meanwhile, I was becoming more ambulatory in the hospital. Strolling on the veranda one day, I was greeted by an elderly gentleman. "Hello, how are you feeling today?"

"Better, thank you," I responded. "My name is Lovestrand."

"I'm Sukarni," he answered, and we shook hands.

"You probably know about me. I'm a prisoner."

"Yes, but your guard is gone now. Mine are still here," and he motioned toward two MPs sitting down by his room.

"Maybe they thought it was unnecessary to have a separate guard for me when there are already two MPs here watching you," I suggested.

"No, I asked them about this," Mr. Sukarni replied. "They told me that they have no orders at all to guard you, so you see you have more freedom than I."

Gradually I learned his story. He had been a close friend of Mr. Sukarno's during the revolution against the Dutch. Mr. Sukarni was a leader of the Murba Party, which I understand was leftist. It followed somewhat the ideas of Trotsky rather than Lenin. From 1961 through 1963 he was the Indonesian ambassador to Peking. Upon his return to his own country, he had warned the president that the Communist Party of Indonesia (PKI) was plotting his downfall, assisted by Peking.

His reward for this helpful advice was to be thrown in jail for subverting the Communist Party. Now he was allowed to stay in the hospital because of high blood pressure and sugar diabetes.

One day he said, "Do you know why there has been so much propaganda over the radio and in the newspapers against the United States and the CIA?"

My ears pricked up. "Why?" I inquired.

"It is clear now that the Communists were training a small but secret army at Lubang Buaja for many months. They had been planning their coup for a much longer period. The propaganda campaign against the United States was organized to draw attention away from their own dirty work. You, of course, fitted beautifully into the picture. They could build you up as a dangerous spy and the angered people of Indonesia would demand your punishment."

In the middle of February, word came to me that the reason why the American Embassy had not yet been able to secure my release was that some Indonesian officials were recommending to the president that instead of a quick and quiet release my case should be brought to trial. This meant that probably Dr. Subandrio in the Foreign Ministry was holding my case up. As long as I might be useful to him, as long as there was a chance that the Communists could regain their power, I would be held.

When Muriel brought me the news of the possibility of a trial, we wondered how this could possibly bring glory to the Lord. Surely if there were a public trial, with all of the accounts printed in the daily newspapers, there would be many who would believe the reports, who would sincerely believe that a Christian missionary had actually been involved in some sort of illegal activity. How could this help the cause of Christian missions?

"I was told that if you were tried, you would be found guilty, then given a suspended sentence and deported," Muriel said.

"But I haven't even been charged with anything yet," I answered. "It seems to me that if Subandrio is interested in hanging on to me there must be other people in the government who are equally interested in letting me go. He certainly isn't popular in some circles."

"I know," Muriel said. "Riding back and forth on the bus I see the signs that are painted all over town, 'Subandrio is a dog from Peking,' 'Get Rid of Subandrio,' and even 'Hang Subandrio.'"

By this time we were talking in whispers. It was difficult not to feel that someone was eavesdropping on everything we said.

"The ambassador is back in Washington for consultations," Muriel told me.

"I was listening on the radio the other night and heard a speech by Sukarno. In the background were shouts of '*Usir* Green, *Usir* Green' ('Chase out Green'). The Communist element want to get rid of him and chase him out."

"That's the element that is trying to keep you in," Muriel said. "Mr. Diefenbach has been to me to see about getting $1,000 from the mission for a lawyer and court costs. I told him that I could advance this from our account if it were urgent, and that I could work it out with the mission later."

"Let's pray it doesn't come to that," I said.

Others were concerned that a trial be avoided. Cindy Adams was one of them. A newspaper columnist, she became acquainted with President Sukarno. Then she wrote his biography and he was so flattered by this that she believed he would do her a favor. Wanting to ask him for my release, she decided to talk to Muriel first and get the facts of the case.

Joe Jimmerson, a Southern Baptist missionary, drove Muriel over to meet Mrs. Adams. "Both my husband and I will be spending the weekend at the summer palace in Bogor. I hope that this will give me an opportunity to speak to the president about Mr. Lovestrand," she said.

Muriel told her what had happened when Pat Price made her try. "Please be careful, and don't press him too hard," she pleaded.

"I'll be careful," she promised.

25

Prayer Is the Answer

When Cindy Adams and her husband Joey strolled into the gaily-lit reception hall of the summer palace, Cindy's eyes searched the place for the president. As it turned out, it was Dr. Subandrio, the Foreign Minister, and not Mr. Sukarno whom she confronted.

Seeing the couple, Dr. Subandrio beckoned to them to join his circle, and soon they were all in animated conversation. Dr. Subandrio, a witty and polished man, threw compliments at his attractive American guest. With a courtly gesture he told her, "Now, Mrs. Adams, if there is ever anything I can do for you—anything at all—be sure to let me know, and I will be glad to take care of it for you."

This was an unexpected but welcome opening. Cindy seized full advantage of it. "Well," she replied, "as a matter of fact, there is something you can do for me."

Others lifted their heads to follow the conversation, and Dr. Subandrio noticed that he had a big audience. Anxious to make a good impression, he asked, "What is it?"

"You know that missionary that you are holding?"

"What missionary?" Dr. Subandrio replied, much taken aback.

"You know whom I mean!"

"You mean Lovestrand?"

"Of course. You're not holding any other missionaries, are you?"

"No."

"Well, why don't you let him go?"

There was silence for a moment as the whole group around them fixed their eyes on Dr. Subandrio and waited for his answer. Then he looked up and said abruptly, "All right, I will."

"Now look," Mrs. Adams continued, "here you sit in front of all these people calmly telling me that you are going to release him. You'd better not be kidding me."

"I'm not. I mean it."

Cindy Adams was well aware of Dr. Subandrio's reputation for broken promises, so she looked him straight in the eye and asked, "When?"

He tried to evade the issue, but she brought him back to the question again and again, until finally, embarrassed by this public entrapment, he gave her his promise.

"You come in on Tuesday morning, and I'll have the papers ready," he said.

Muriel had this story relayed to her on Sunday night after the Adamses returned to the city, and she told me about it when she came to visit on Monday.

"I don't have much faith that he'll keep his promise," I said.

"I don't either," Muriel said, "but Mrs. Adams certainly tried her best."

The next morning I was listening to the regular Djakarta news broadcast in Indonesian and heard the announcement that Mrs. Adams had paid a visit to Dr.

Subandrio. Nothing was said about the purpose of her visit.

The days that followed moved slowly. I waited and wondered, but still no further news came. Finally on Sunday evening Mr. Diefenbach visited me. At least he relieved the suspense, but all he could offer was in the negative. Dr. Subandrio had no intention of keeping his promise. Mrs. Adams had only received a vague answer from him. Another disappointment for us! I told Muriel, "We ought to have learned by this time not to get our hopes up with each promise of a release."

"It will be a disappointment to a lot of other people too," she said. "We need to be ready for God's answer at anytime."

We shared a recent letter from Tim from boarding school in the Philippines. He started, "I guess I don't pray about Dad's situation as much as I ought. When I read your letter I couldn't help feeling rather depressed at the seemingly endless runabout and delay. But I guess that prayer is the answer." Then by the end of the letter he had in block letters, "PRAYER IS THE ANSWER!" written over six times, and then, "the answer to prayer is imminent!" He underlined the last word five times, and in spite of our seemingly stalled position, it made me feel mighty good.

The letter helped take our minds off the crowded restive city of Djakarta for a few moments and wing over in imagination to Manila.

The Indonesian students were rampaging on the streets of Djakarta, angered at the way inflation was touching them. In December the Indonesian currency had changed. Now rice was thirty times what it had been a year earlier. Runaway prices accompanied the spiraling inflation. The rupiah exchange rate soared crazily to 50,000 to an American dollar.

University students in Djakarta, the educational center of the islands, found it almost impossible to buy books. Then tuition was raised and this was the last straw.

The students were aroused as never before. They saw that after twenty years of independence their country was bankrupt, the populace was not getting enough to eat, officials often had a reputation for being easily bribed, the country seemed to be betrayed to the Communists and the president was still blind to the danger even after the Communists were revealed as brutal killers. He seemed indifferent to the sufferings of his disillusioned people.

The university students belonging to a student federation called KAMI (University Students Union for Action) staged demonstrations in the street demanding:

1. The abolition of the Partai Komunis Indonesia
2. Reduction of prices
3. Formation of a new, smaller cabinet.

They wrote slogans on the walls, halted traffic and presented petitions. These measures seemed so futile, because seemingly nothing had any effect on the executive branch of government where Sukarno still kept his old cronies around him. Ill-advisedly, he took too bold a step by firing popular General Nasution on February 21. This was a shock to us, for we had seen General Nasution several times when he came to the hospital for treatment. President Sukarno had issued a challenge to all anti-Communists, which they promptly seized.

On February 23, the students held a gigantic demonstration. They moved in the streets toward the presidential palace, an area which had been forbidden to them. Armed guards tried to hold them back, but they were surging forward from every direction.

Another group moved toward the Office of the Foreign Minister, Dr. Subandrio, to shout their hatred, to hang him in effigy, eventually to overrun and ransack the offices in their anger at not finding him.

Muriel, unaware of what was going on, visited me this day. I had heard rumors that the students were demonstrating, but this did not seem so unusual. Muriel had brought me food and she stayed and talked with me as I ate. Then shortly before one o'clock, she went home.

In about an hour I heard the sound of gunfire. I rushed to the edge of the veranda with other patients. The shots came from only a block away. We listened and speculated. Then we heard more shots, this time coming from the direction of the president's palace. We wondered what was going on, figuring that in some way the students and the armed guards must have met and faced each other.

Around three o'clock in the afternoon, we heard a great uproar, the sound of many voices, coming closer and closer. It mounted in intensity. It came from outside the hospital gates.

We strained to see.

"Are the demonstrators here at the hospital?"

"Yes, at least some of them are. See, there are the yellow sweaters of the university students. Look, see them crowded around that truck."

The pavilion was so placed that from one corner we had a good view of the emergency entrance and ward. We could see a jumble of cars and jeeps arriving, crowded to the hilt.

"Hey, they're carrying a student."

We saw someone being lifted down and carried into the emergency operating room. There was another casualty, limping, half-carried by fellow students. Others were brought in. Shouts of anger rent the air. The students who had flowed into the hospital courtyard looked stunned, bewildered, enraged. Some of them shouted orders. Others carried the bloody shirts of their fallen comrades and waved them high for all to see. I counted eight wounded students but heard later that there were nine.

The hours passed. The students in the streets did not go home. They were determined to have vengeance. We heard that thousands of them were still standing outside the presidential palace, as close as the guards would let them. They completely surrounded it and watched carefully to see who might try to come or go.

They had heard that Mr. Sukarno was planning to install a new cabinet the next day. The angry students were determined that this new cabinet, already appointed, should not take office. They were there to prevent this. The president had chosen Communists for some of the vital posts in government, and the students were determined to block him.

26

Students vs. Subandrio

Early the next morning, those of us staying in the hospital heard that the students were still stationed in the strategic streets leading to the palace. Automobiles and trucks were stopped. They let the air out of their tires. Traffic was snarled, and it looked as if it would be impossible for the new cabinet to be installed by President Sukarno.

We could hear the shouts of students and occasionally a dull roar of massed voices. The air was tense, and patients discussed what turn events might take. Some of them had ugly premonitions that somehow the government would outmaneuver the university students.

"What's that?" one of the patients called.

Then we heard the *clop-clop-clop* of helicopters. They flew over the hospital in a steady line, one passing every two minutes.

"They look like army helicopters, or are they air force?" someone asked.

They were olive drab, but they could have been either from the army or air force. Skimming over the roofs and streets, they passed over the barricades, while the youth shook their fists at them. The whirlybirds went on until they landed in the palace grounds.

President Sukarno and Dr. Subandrio had figured out a way to outsmart the KAMI organizers. They had collected most of the new ministers and brought them into the palace by helicopter. One minister, Brigadier General Sokendro, arrived at the palace by bicycle, the only way he could get through. The students had let him pass because he was in uniform.

In one way or another most of the ministers got through and Mr. Sukarno began the installation of the cabinet. He addressed his supporters in a belligerent mood. Denouncing the students, he declared, "I am a leader who can't be pushed. Don't push me, or you'll see what happens!"

In the streets and the public squares the students were boiling with rage and resentment. Insulted, outfoxed, smarting from frustration, they decided in a passionate rage to storm the palace. They broke through the outer defense perimeter and moved in closer. The soldiers were helpless to stem the flood.

Suddenly a jeep loaded with soldiers of the *Tjakrabirawa* (the palace guard) drove headlong into the maddened throng. The students hurled rocks at the vehicle and smashed the windshield. Blood ran down the face of one of the soldiers. Then the marines defending the palace charged the students. In the ensuing melee shots rang out. Burp guns blasted their deadly lead. Automatic rifles joined the crackling fire.

The shots startled me in my hospital room. I walked out to the veranda. The firing came from two directions, some of it from the large, open park in front of the palace and some of the trouble was evidently close to the palace itself.

It was about 11 o'clock in the morning. After listening

awhile, I returned to my room and lay down. There I prayed while I continued to hear shots echoing and reechoing. The shooting was much more intense than the previous day. Then it occurred to me that Muriel might attempt to visit me at the hospital, unaware of the rioting and bloodshed. She might travel in from the suburb of Kebajoran Baru and not run into trouble until near the hospital. Going to one of the doctors, I requested that he phone Muriel and advise her to stay home. This he did, and I returned to my room, happy and relieved.

It was about lunchtime when crowds of students again arrived at the hospital gates. They brought in their wounded comrades, and those of us on the upper veranda of the pavilion had a grandstand view. The noise and commotion was contagious. So many students were milling around that I could only guess at the number of wounded they brought in. Then the word spread like wildfire that a medical student at the University of Indonesia, Arif Rachman Hakim, had been killed!

The next day was a sad one. The city seemed hushed for the funeral procession of young Arif. The funeral procession started at the university, headquarters for KAMI, and thousands followed the coffin to the cemetery. There the students showed that though they were saddened they were not vanquished. One after another vowed that Arif had not died in vain. A wife of one of the generals killed by the Communists on October 1 also addressed the students, and they were reminded afresh by this widow's presence of what the Communists would do if they were ever permitted to regain power.

It was clear from the speeches that Arif in his death had given the students a hero and a martyr to personify their struggle against the pro-Communist forces in government. The government had struck at them, and they were determined to strike back. This was revolutionary. With renewed courage, the students dedicated themselves to fight for a clean, respectable government.

President Sukarno was well aware of the dangers in these student uprisings. He closeted with his advisors and on February 26 he decreed that KAMI be banned and dissolved. Now what were the students going to do? If they continued their demonstrations, the government would arrest the KAMI leaders and throw them into jail.

For a few days, there was a lull in demonstrations. Everybody in the city was wondering what was going to happen next.

The KAMI leadership decided on a new strategy, and they called on the high school student federation, KAP-PI, to take over the outward leadership of the student revolt. The junior and senior high school students were itching to have a part in demonstrations. Even grade school students wanted to participate and many high school teachers were glad to encourage the younger students to go out on the march. School was suspended. Former members of KAMI infiltrated KAPPI to give it leadership. In the hospital I heard allegations that some of the military, clothed in civilian garb, also were loaned to KAPPI. It was no secret that the army sympathized with the students, but on the surface they remained neutral.

Meanwhile, it was rumored that the hated Dr. Suban-drio, whom the students suspected of having a major part in the October coup, was making a bold but hazardous gamble. Using his position as close confidant and advisor of the president, he was said to have written Mr.

Sukarno a secret letter. In it he suggested that the president fire General Suharto, army chief of staff, just as he had fired General Nasution, and then he suggested that both generals be tried by a special military court for the death of thousands of Communists in the months following their unsuccessful bid for power.

Rumors were rife. Both sides realized that the impasse could not continue indefinitely. Someone would emerge the winner; the other would be the loser.

On March 3, it was KAPPI's turn to strike. All over the city students wrote their slogans and stopped traffic. They let air out of tires and blocked the streets. They wrote on the sides of buses, automobiles and trucks. Their most popular slogans were, "Make prices come down," "Dismiss the cabinet," "Hang Subandrio."

Communists were sneaking out and writing slogans too. One large one said, "Go to Hell, Green." But usually their slogans were painted over quickly. The army arrested any Communist sign painters they could find. On the contrary, the students who favored Generals Nasution and Suharto found that army guards looked the other way when they were busy with their paintbrushes.

Thousands of younger students marched on the Office of Basic Education, demanding that Minister Sumardjo be ousted as a Communist sympathizer. Somehow KAPPI had secured trucks and brought in loads of shouting, singing youngsters. These masses of students tried to seize the ministry office. Others converged on the Ministry of Foreign Affairs, where Dr. Subandrio had his office.

From my hospital room I again heard the *rat-a-tat-tat* of machine guns and the sound of automatic rifles. I shuddered and wondered who was being wounded or killed this time.

Would another crowd of students bring their wounded friends to the hospital? I waited and waited to see. After several hours, when things had quieted down, and none had come, I breathed a prayer of thanks to God.

The next morning's newspaper told me that Dr. Subandrio had not been at the Ministry of Foreign Affairs. The students wanted to present a copy of their demands and resolutions to him in person. Failing this, they lowered the flag at the ministry to half-mast in memory of their martyred hero, Arif.

When the army had been called on to disperse the mobs, their answer had been, "What can we do? We can't shoot a bunch of children. Why they even lie down in front of our armored cars!"

An army officer who was a patient at the hospital was able to go out and see what was happening. When he came back in, he said to me, "You ought to see the park square in front of the Ministry of Foreign Affairs! Papers are strewn all around. It looks like it has snowed there. The students went into the offices and ransacked them. They threw out all the files they could find. They smashed tables, chairs and windows. What a mess it is! And outside the ministry, the students have placed a big picture. It is a picture of a dog with the head of Dr. Subandrio. There is a chain leading from the collar of the dog, and this is held by a Chinese. Underneath it says, 'Bandrio, dog of Peking!'"

27

Sukarno Yields

Dr. Subandrio was not idle. "You must take the initiative," he told President Sukarno, and he began to outline what could be done. On March 8, the president addressed some of his supporters at the Bung Karno Sports Stadium. Later I listened to a rebroadcast of his speech over my roommate's radio. It came over at 8:05 that evening from Radio Djakarta.

I heard the familiar bellowing voice, *"Baris! Baris! Baris dibelakang Sukarno!"* ("Line up! Line up! Line up in back of Sukarno!")

This was familiar language. I had heard it in previous speeches. Dr. Subandrio on several instances had tried to start a new movement of all parties called *Barisan Sukarno* ("the Sukarno Front"). This would have been a repetition of *Nasakom,* giving the Communists a hiding place. But the army would have none of it. They declared that they had already lined up in back of President Sukarno, and that the pro-Communist forces were anti-Sukarno.

The president continued his speech, trying to fan anti-American spirit. He condemned the United States and all the rest of the "imperialists" and "colonialists." His audience let out screams, "Chase out Green! Chase out Green!" It sounded like a spontaneous and lively response, but I felt sure that it had been staged. The government wanted the people of Djakarta to believe that it had wide, public support.

Muriel was able to visit me the next day, March 9, though I was concerned about her coming into the heart of the city under these conditions. I listened hungrily for every word she had about events outside, while I was able to share with her some news which I had gotten from my fellow patients and their visitors. She told me that she had heard of a crowd of three hundred or so pro-Communists demonstrating in front of the American Embassy. The demonstrators had forced their way inside the gates and burned four or five cars. Some of them had even gained entrance to one of the rooms, bringing out books and papers and burning them. The American marines kept them from doing more damage inside and eventually they dispersed. Subandrio must have felt that this partially countered the wrecking of his offices.

KAPPI, with its KAMI backing, did not delay its retaliation. The next morning at six they were gathered and ready to move—their objective the Communist China Embassy. Between 2,000 and 3,000 stormed the place, but the walls were very high and a high barbed wire fence was on top of the wall.

A visitor to the hospital told a group of us what happened. When the students saw that it was virtually impossible to knock down the gates, they spied a steamroller nearby. One of the laborers in a road repair crew volunteered to ram the gates of the embassy with the steamroller. *Smash!* The gates gave way. The students let out a cheer and rushed in. A few were injured by the Chinese guards, but the number of students simply overwhelmed the Chinese. Entering the embassy, they grabbed furniture, files, and equipment and hurled these outside. The Chinese guards continued to struggle with the students, but they found that they received as much or more than they gave. Those who hurt the students found that the students practiced an eye-for-an-eye, tooth-for-a-tooth philosophy. Soon a bonfire in the entry-way was merrily licking at the pile of debris.

Other students rushed off to the Chinese Trade Commission Office. This was also a heavily protected building, but the students borrowed a military jeep, and following the method used at the Chinese Embassy, smashed through the gates surrounding the trade office. The Chinese guards there had iron bars which they brandished in an effort to hurl the students back. It was useless. The mob surged in. They burned cars and wrecked the offices.

Next it was the turn of the New China News Agency. They sacked this propaganda center of the Communists and started a fire in the building. I heard the fire engines screaming by as they went to put out the blaze.

The offices of the Partai Komunis Indonesia were burned, and my sources said that it was done with gasoline borrowed from the army. The home of Communist leader Aidit went up in flames, and the excited students kept on looking for other targets on which to vent their fury.

I saw a copy of an Indonesian newspaper which carried a picture of President Sukarno viewing the damage at the Office of Foreign Affairs. He was quoted as saying at the time of his visit, "This is not just a political game any more. This is a counter-revolution."

An old hand like Mr. Sukarno certainly could recognize

the power that had been unleashed, but now instead of being the revolutionary leader, he was trying to stem the tide. That was not nearly as easy.

The students continued their demonstrations with mounting enthusiasm. Traffic was snarled. They took over gasoline stations and sold gas at its former price. They streamed into offices and banks. They threatened merchants as to what would happen to them unless prices dropped. They continued to clash with the presidential guards in the palace area. I would still hear shots in the daytime and sometimes shattering the still of the night. We patients speculated as to what the end of it all would be.

Finally President Sukarno summoned the leaders of the political parties to the presidential palace on March 10. He gave them an ultimatum. They must sign and issue a statement branding the University of Indonesia and the Technological Institute of Bandung as counter-revolutionary centers and the members of the Student Action Organizations as counter-revolutionaries.

The political leaders refused to comply with this order. Then Dr. Subandrio got up and threatened them with arrest unless they complied with the president's request. The political leaders wavered and eventually signed a compromise statement stating that they could not agree with the methods employed by the students. They said that rioting would undermine the authority of the president, *Pemimpin Besar Revolusi Kita*, ("Our Great Leader of the Revolution"). Dr. Subandrio was pleased and rushed the statement to the press.

When the newspapers printed what the political leaders had signed, the students exploded. They rushed to these leaders and demanded that they retract what they had said. This they quickly did, issuing new statements explaining that they had not had sufficient time to study and discuss the question, that they had been under pressure to sign before thinking through all the implications of the declaration.

In this state of confusion the president called his cabinet together once more. The students learned through sympathetic officers in government that the meeting was called for six o'clock the morning of March 11. Mr. Sukarno intended to avoid the students by the early meeting. To his chagrin the students were alerted the night before and stood guard outside the homes of the various ministers. When morning came some of the ministers were held in their homes, while others decided to change their plans. Some ministers did manage to get through to the palace by helicopter, but Mr. Sukarno did not have a quorum.

He waited until ten o'clock, hoping that more of the ministers would arrive, and then, grim-faced, he opened the meeting. That evening I heard a rebroadcast of a speech by the president over Radio Djakarta. In his usual persuasive manner, he tried to convince his listeners that he knew his job, that only he could hold the country together. He condemned the methods, slogans and demands of the students. He ridiculed what he called their juvenile thinking and juvenile conduct. I put my ear closer to the radio. I didn't want to miss any of this.

Then suddenly his speech stopped. I called to my room-mate, "Hey, did you hear the end of that speech? The president didn't say, '*Sekianlah*' ("The end"). He didn't come to a formal conclusion. Everything was left hanging. Did you hear that? Something is in the wind."

My room-mate, who had been half-dozing, said, "Ah, you're just imagining things. There was nothing wrong."

"No," I insisted, "there is something wrong. It was as if he was almost cut off. It didn't end like it usually does. I heard him say something like, '*Uh, apa itu?*" ("Uh, what's that?") Then he handed the cabinet meeting over to Dr. Leimena. There's something funny about the way the speech ended."

And I was right. The next day the story came through the hospital grapevine. Some soldiers, stripped of all insignia and markings, surrounded the palace. I suspected that most of them were from the RPKAD, the army commandos. While the president was giving his address, one of his aides, Sumirat, entered. He handed a note to the president. It read, "There is a company of unmarked soldiers surrounding the palace to kidnap the president."

The president lost his composure. Handing the meeting over to Dr. Leimena, he reached for his coat and left. Dr. Subandrio and Dr. Chairul Saleh, third deputy minister, followed hastily after him.

On his way out, the president said to Brigadier General Amir Mahmud, commander of the Djakarta division, "You are responsible for my safety, the safety of the president."

They rushed out to a waiting helicopter which lifted them up and over the city, and headed for the summer palace at Bogor, forty miles away. In his haste, Dr. Subandrio left his shoes behind, having slipped them off for comfort during the meeting.

Dr. Leimena adjourned the meeting, and then some ministers who were favorable to the army hurried over to General Suharto's headquarters. When General Suharto heard what had happened he immediately dispatched Generals Amir Mahmud, Andi Jusuf and Basuki Rachmat to Bogor to hand the president an ultimatum. They went with a task force and reaching Bogor, confronted Sukarno.

"This is the situation," they said. "Your life is in danger, but we can manage to save you and your teachings of the revolution. The only way, however, is for you, the president, to sign over executive authority to General Suharto, and you must express your confidence in the army."

Dr. Subandrio stepped over to President Sukarno, "Don't do it," he warned.

General Mahmud (whose wife was a patient in the pavilion of the hospital where I was located), tersely ordered Dr. Subandrio to be silent. *"Djangan tjampur tangan!"* ("Don't you meddle!") he said.

One of the generals said to Mr. Sukarno, "Right now there are mobs of students surrounding the summer palace. Do you hear them? Do you know why they are coming in? They want to get you. We can't control them much longer. If you don't submit to the will of the people, we'll have to leave you to the mobs."

Mr. Sukarno wilted. Reluctantly he signed the prepared paper the generals had brought to him. It gave all authority to General Suharto to rule and make decrees in his name.

Over the radio that night the armed forces were ordered to gather the next morning at the Bung Karno Stadium. It was announced as a "Show of Force." The news spread like wildfire all over Djakarta, and the stadium was full. When the news was announced that General Suharto was in control, a parade began which threaded its way from the stadium back into the city.

Hilarious soldiers and students rode along, arms linked together, shouting and hooting. The streets along the way were jampacked with spectators, reaching out to shake their hands. Some people threw fruit up to the men on vehicles for them to eat. The skins of fruit littered the streets afterward. Djakarta had never before seen such a victory march. The students had won. The army who supported them was now in control.

The celebration spread to the hospital, and judging by the excitement around me, what was it like in the streets? The first order General Suharto made in the name of the president was to dissolve the PKI and ban any and all of its acitvities.

Dr. Subandrio was soon out of office and another man appointed in his place. I knew this would certainly have some personal bearing on my case.

However, another problem began to loom. The hospital authorities had declared me completely well and were unwilling for me to stay there and use a much needed bed any longer. They insisted that I be discharged. But if I was to leave the hospital, where would I go? As a prisoner I could only go back to prison.

Hearing of this difficulty, the embassy officials swung into action to help me. Muriel worked with them, holding to the hope that the prison would now be so full of Communists that there would not be room for me. I told her that if I had to go back to prison that at least I felt well enough physically to face it.

Muriel would have none of it. "I don't want you going back there," she said. "We're going to try and get you placed under some sort of house arrest."

28

The Real Thing?

"Good morning, Mrs. Lovestrand," Mr. *Diefenbach* greeted Muriel on Monday, March 14, at the embassy. "The worst of the riots seem to be over, and the streets are clear. Did you have any difficulty getting here?"

"No, the buses are running again, and I got through without any problem," Muriel replied.

"Well, I doubt if anything has been done one way or the other in regard to moving Mr. Lovestrand from the hospital. The officials will all be waiting to see how the latest developments are going to affect policy. This waiting period will probably be a good time to file our request with the Public Prosecutor's Department that he not be returned to prison."

They went out to an embassy car which took them over to the Justice Department. They could sense a new attitude in the men they approached about the case. They, too, expressed that they were anxious to prevent my being moved back to prison.

"The investigation was satisfactorily completed in December, and it is completely unnecessary from our point of view for Mr. Lovestrand to be detained further," Mr. Soederadjat said. "We must work out some other plan. I know what we can do! We will arrange for papers placing him under house arrest after he is discharged from the hospital. It will take a bit of time to get the papers ready, so please come back, Mr. Diefenbach, say on Wednesday. I'll have them ready for you then."

Mr. Diefenbach returned on March 16, only to be told, "We don't have the papers. We've decided not to place Mr. Lovestrand under house arrest."

"Oh, is that so?" exclaimed Mr. Diefenbach.

"Yes," said Mr. Soederadjat, "I've talked with my superiors, and we have decided to grant him a full release instead. He will be free to leave the country immediately."

"That's fine," said Mr. Diefenbach, "but what are you going to do about the hospital situation? The superintendent there has already signed his release papers and wants his bed as soon as possible."

"I'll take care of that," he replied. "We'll phone the hospital authorities to hold on to him a few days longer until we get our papers ready. Be sure that you don't tell Lovestrand that he will be released shortly. And by all means, don't tell your ambassador. Ambassadors have a way of getting excited over things like this!"

Mr. Diefenbach found the embassy medical officer, Dr. Woods, and went to see the hospital authorities. He wanted to be sure that there would be no slip up and that they understood what the Public Prosecutor's Department was planning.

The superintendent called the Public Prosecutor's Department, exchanged a few words in Javanese, and then agreed to the proposal. I would be able to continue temporarily at the hospital.

Mr. Diefenbach drove out to tell Muriel about the new

prospects for my release, and she could hardly believe that it might be true.

"Do you think it's the real thing this time?" she asked.

"It looks like the real thing," Mr. Diefenbach replied. "You noticed how much more helpful the officials appeared when you went with me on Monday. I believe that Subandrio's fall makes all the difference. I advise you to start packing, but don't tell anyone yet. We'll have to keep it quiet until we actually have the release papers in hand."

Muriel started the round of packing again, being careful not to do it when anyone else was around. It seemed hard to believe, yet she knew that sometime would be the last time. She couldn't tell the children yet. And it wouldn't do to return any of the borrowed household furnishings.

On March 18 we heard that Dr. Subandrio had been placed under arrest. A new Foreign Affairs minister had been appointed.

Muriel and I were discussing this in the hospital on March 21.

"Do you think the release will come through this time?" I asked.

"It's hard to say," she replied. "They've promised so many times before. I do believe that the Lord is going to take us out of here and that it won't be much longer."

She showed me a recent letter from Tim and said, "Your imprisonment has been a blessing in his life."

I looked at the letter. It was written from Faith Academy in Manila on March 12. Tim told us more about the spiritual revival among the students and how gospel teams were being greatly used in open-air evangelism.

He wrote:

Today we got an item from AP that Sukarno handed his power to Suharto. That's a big enough piece of news, isn't it? I certainly hope that you and the rest of the family will be able to come soon, but I am sure that the Lord still has some things to teach me. I think I told you before that the Lord told me that you wouldn't be able to come until I let Him teach me a few things. Just pray that I will always be willing to let Him teach me these things.

"I certainly hope that the Lord will complete everything He is doing through my imprisonment, so I can get out," I said. "It's so complex. So much is tied in with what has happened to us. People have been praying for us, and they begin to learn about the problems of Indonesia. They pray for the country, and a Communist takeover is averted. The Lord holds me longer, and the people at home continue to pray. And a good thing, too, for the Communists have been trying to get back into power. Now their prayers are answered for the country.

"More than that, because they pray for us, they also pray for our children. We see the Lord do a new work in their hearts and lives. Praying for Tim and Andrea gets them praying for Faith Academy. We'll never know just where it ends."

Muriel left me later, planning to return to the embassy. On arrival there she waited in the library until Mr. Diefenbach would be free to see her. After a while the door opened, and he strode in, carrying a brown envelope. He handed it to Muriel with the words, *"Bebas!* ('Free') Congratulations!"

Muriel stared for a moment at the envelope in disbelief. Free? Did he really mean it? The official release
actually in her hands? She slit the envelope open hurriedly, and there was the long-awaited paper.

Immediately they got an embassy car and came over
to the hospital to share the good news with me. I was
taking a siesta when they walked in. Rubbing my eyes, I
looked at the government order for my deportation. I
read it over carefully:

> The above named person is to leave the country as
> quickly as possible and is forbidden to return as long as
> there is no other decision.

This order was being distributed to ten different government offices concerned with my case. I looked at the
signatures. Yes, at last our prayers and the prayers of
thousands of others had been answered. Here was my
passport to freedom.

We began to make plans for a quick departure. Mr.
Diefenbach said that he would get in touch with Mr.
Neigenfind of the Associated Missions office to arrange
for the first possible plane out of the country in any
direction—Singapore, Bangkok, Hongkong or Manila. I
was given only forty-eight hours in which to leave.

Muriel was now free to finish packing and do the
cleaning that was necessary in her temporary home. The
next day was a Tuesday, and she came to the hospital to
bring me a change of clothes for the trip. "The first flight
that can take all of us is tomorrow," she said. "The
Public Prosecutor's Department people will take you to
the airport."

She showed me a note that she had received from an

Indonesian neighbor with whom she had become acquainted out in Kebajoran Baru:

> Wishing you a happy trip ... may your family always be happy. If we have erred, please forgive us.

"The Indonesians don't want us to go away with any bitterness about our experience," she said. "I hope that they can see that we don't hold any grudge against them."

Wednesday morning, March 23, held a special excitement for me as I sat waiting with my few things ready. God had been so good to me and to my family.

Mr. Diefenbach came in. "Have you seen any of the Public Prosecutor's Department officials?" he asked.

"No, they haven't come here," I replied.

He went to investigate. Evidently the hospital authorities expected them to come, while the Public Prosecutor's Department said to send me over to their building. Finally the hospital allowed me to go with an MP to the Public Prosecutor's Department. Mr. Soederadjat sent him back, and from that point I was through with armed guards. An escort, yes, but not a guard.

Edging through the snarled noontime traffic, our Public Prosecutor's Department car slowed down, and I saw another car threading its way through the traffic jam. In it were Mr. and Mrs. Lay of The Christian and Missionary Alliance, my wife and the four children! We met at the airport, went through formalities at the counter and then had a considerable wait.

Mr. Prasetyo had accompanied Mr. Soederadjat and myself to the airport. These men wanted to be sure that I didn't hold those interrogations against them.

"I hope that you don't hate us because of what you went through," one of them said.

"No, I love the Indonesian people and hope that I may have the opportunity to come back again," I replied. I didn't have to pretend. I spoke from my heart. "This is a beautiful place. It's like my second country I've been here so long."

"Please notice, Mr. Lovestrand, that the deportation notice doesn't say forever and ever. Another decision could be made in your favor. We need men like you to teach our people about God. I hope that some day after things settle down a bit in our country that you will come back again."

This assurance was repeated several times. As we got ready to board the KLM plane for Singapore and Bangkok, Mr. Soederadjat repeated this, "Notice that there is a loophole. Another decision could be reached. The door is not closed. You are leaving now, but it is not final that you cannot come back. I hope that you will."

We said good-by to him and to the missionary friends who had come to see us off. Inside the plane we found our seats were toward the front, and I settled back to relax. The children had begged to be by the windows. I didn't get a view of the palm trees and red tile roofs as we lifted off the ground, just a glimpse of the *Puntjak* in the distance as we turned northward to freedom.

Nearing Bangkok, I said to Muriel, "We ought to get a cable off to the mission. Do you have any paper handy? I'll write one out."

I opened my Bible and searched for a verse that would express just how we felt.

"I'm going to send Isaiah 55:12," I told Muriel, "Listen

to it: 'For ye shall go out in joy, and be led forth with peace . . .' Isn't that good?"

"Yes, it's one of the promises the Lord has fulfilled," she said.

Then I wrote my message:

GOD FULFILLING ISAIAH FIFTY FIVE TWELVE STOP LEFT DJAKARTA THREE OCLOCK TWENTY THIRD STOP PROCEEDING HONG KONG MANILA AND STAYING UNTIL SCHOOL OUT END OF APRIL STOP HEARTFELT THANKS TO ALL WHO PRAYED STOP

"Look at all those 'stops'," I said to Muriel. "I've got another 'stop' to put in there." And I added,

DON'T STOP PRAYING

HAROLD

"It's over, and yet it isn't over," I mused. "God has finished with what He had to teach me and you and Tim and others out of this, and yet He's going to teach us more. God has finished the witness to embassy officials, Indonesian officials, MPs and prisoners, but we're going to go on witnessing."

"Just think, the Bible school has started again at Saowi," Muriel said.

"I wish I could be there, but right now I'm just glad to be here," I replied.

"Together," she murmured, reaching for my hand.

"Yes, dear," I answered. "Together with God!"

29

By Life or by Death

A letter from Holland in the mail! I did not recognize the name of the writer. Good news had been coming from Indonesia as one after another of my fellow prisoners was set free. Sultan Hamid Alkadrie who had said "just call me Max" had written a cheerful letter after his release. Colonel Nikolas Simbolon, leader of the Christian services in prison, walked out a free man during the early summer. Within a year of the attempted take-over by the Communist party another type of revolution had swept Indonesia, a return to reason and justice and faith.

I slit the letter open, wondering what it could be about. My eyes caught the first lines, and a shock wave hit me:

> I am sorry to inform you that Dr. Christian Soumokil, L.L.D. . . . has been executed, shot dead by a firing squad on a little island called Ubi, in the bay of Djakarta, on the morning of the 12th of April, 7 o'clock.

No, no, it couldn't be! My mind rejected the idea, all the time recognizing the futility of my dismay. There was the letter. Thank God that the lawyer who had written it, Dr. Soumokil's lawyer, did more than give me the information with polite regrets. He had obviously been a close friend to my friend and had labored in vain to save his life. He wrote:

> Chris refused to be blindfolded with the usual black mask and asked not to be tied to the pole. Then, after praying with the Protestant chaplain, Chris himself ordered the shooting, "I am ready; shoot now!"

The authorities who carried out his death sentence must have treated him with respect at the last. He had to die, but Dr. Soumokil died with dignity. I was glad of that. It is the way he would have wanted it.

So he was ready! Yes, I knew he was ready. When I left him for the last time, I was being carried out on a stretcher. I had said, *"Pak,*" if we never meet again here on earth, I'll be looking forward to seeing you in heaven."

On that occasion I wasn't thinking of his going to meet the Lord first. I was seriously wondering how much longer I might have on this earth.

My imagination whirled through scenes I had not witnessed—*Pak* Soumokil being called from his cell in the isolation block to a waiting automobile, guards taking him to a pier, then riding three hours aboard a launch to Ubi Island, and finally arriving at the place of execution. The sentence of "death by a firing squad" pronounced two years before was being carried out. What would he have done? My mind steadied. I could visualize him in prayer, preparing his soul to meet God, laying aside those dreams of future service in the ministry, praying for his family, for his nation . . . and could it be? . . . for me.

A lump rose in my throat. My eyes burned. How knit together we are in the body of Christ, and it is the love

---

*A term of respect.

of Christ which does this. One could not help but think of chapter 11 of Hebrews:

> Now faith is the substance of things hoped for, the evidence of things not seen . . . by faith . . . waxed valiant in fight, . . . And these all, having obtained a good report through faith, received not the promise: God having provided some better thing for us, that they without us should not be made perfect.

God took *Pak* Soumokil and left others, blessed be God! He is not unmindful of the hundred million souls in Indonesia with a need for Jesus Christ. One of His servants today is Colonel Simbolon, who shortly after his release, stood before an international gathering of Christian leaders and pled with them, saying,

> The Indonesian is waiting, waiting for the brother who will point him to the way of the true riches of redemption and salvation in Jesus Christ. The moment to act, to seize this God-given opportunity, is now!

Col. Simbolon rehearsed the history of Communist build-up in his country, the abortive coup, the bloody aftermath and the rising, new hopes. He spoke in a spirit of penitence:

> We Indonesian Christians, especially those who have come to be recognized as leaders, have failed tragically by Christian standards. During the difficult years we lacked the courage to stand up and be counted as Christ's crusaders . . . because we preferred to compromise and establish ourselves in good, worldly positions. And a great many of us failed because we were overcome by our spiritual emptiness. Our battery was dead, dried up. We realize now that it was only God who came to our

rescue and saved our nation at the crucial moment. His Name be praised!

God came to the rescue of Indonesia. He kept the country open to the gospel, and there is freedom in Indonesia to proclaim the Good News because He interceded.

This is just a beginning. The potential at present is tremendous, but the harvest will not be brought in without willing, skillful workers. Col. Simbolon urged the mobilization of each individual Christian to this task, and it was obvious that he had dedicated himself to have a part in it.

God trained a worker in those prison days. He took an ex-army colonel, a political detainee, and gave him a parish within those four walls. With the Bible as the wellspring, He gave this man a message which he not only preached on Sundays in the prison chapel, but which he lived throughout each tiresome, dragging week.

He was a prisoner of God's love, who brought him to the place in his Christian experience where he could say, "We are overcome by the Lord's goodness."

Yes, Col. Simbolon, the two of us have learned that nothing can separate us from the love of Christ. We learned it in a Djakarta prison, and we tell it to all the world—it is the lordship of Christ which sets men truly free.

DJAKARTA

TJIREBON

BOGOR (President's Country Palace)

TJILOTO
TJIMATJAN
SUKARNAGALI

JAVA

SA

SIA

MANTAN

BALIKPAPAN

Equator

6164
78594

266.09 Lovestrand, Harold
Lov   Hostage in Djakarta

D

W

S

SURABAJA

Miles